FAT QUARTER
ACCESSORIES

25 projects to make from short lengths of fabric

Susie Johns

First published 2020 by
Guild of Master Craftsman Publications Ltd
Castle Place, 166 High Street, Lewes,
East Sussex, BN7 1XU, UK

ISBN 978 1 78494 565 7

A catalogue record for this book is available from the British Library.

Publisher Jonathan Bailey
Production Jim Bulley and Jo Pallett
Senior Project Editor Dominique Page
Editor Sarah Hoggett
Managing Art Editor Gilda Pacitti
Design & Art Direction Wayne Blades
Photographer Neal Grundy
Step photography Susie Johns

Colour origination by GMC Reprographics

Printed and bound in China

A note on measurements
The imperial measurements in these projects are converted from metric. While every attempt has been made to ensure that they are as accurate as possible, some rounding up or down has been inevitable. For this reason, it is always best to stick to one system or the other throughout a project: do not mix metric and imperial units.

CONTENTS

INTRODUCTION

Well-chosen accessories can finish off an outfit with style. But don't just wait for a special occasion like a wedding, a holiday or a day at the races: accessorize your everyday outfits, too. When you make things yourself, it's easy to co-ordinate your hat with your dress, your scarf with your jacket or your earrings with your shirt. It's also a great way of stamping your personality on an outfit by selecting fabrics in your own unique combinations of colour and pattern.

Most sewing enthusiasts manage to accumulate a lot of fabrics, buttons, ribbons and other bits and bobs. When out and about at the shops, at markets, fairs and exhibitions, or browsing online, they also find it hard to resist buying more fabrics to add to their stashes. Accessories, being relatively small, are a brilliant way to use up remnants, scraps of fabric left over from other sewing projects and, of course, fat quarters.

What is a fat quarter? It's a way of cutting a yard or metre of fabric, usually medium-weight cotton, into four useful pieces – and it's a great way of buying fabrics without breaking the bank. The usual way of cutting a quarter of a yard or metre from a length of fabric produces a strip measuring 9 inches (25cm) by the width of the fabric, which is usually 44 or 45 inches (112 or 115cm). A fat quarter is cut in a different way: cut half a yard/metre of fabric, then cut this piece in half, to give you a piece of fabric approximately 18 x 22 inches (46 x 56cm, or sometimes 50 x 56cm). This squarish shape is, for most projects, far more versatile, and buying fat quarters usually makes it possible to buy four different fabrics for the same cost as a yard or metre of a single design.

The 25 practical and stylish projects in this book will help you to make the most of these fat quarters and smaller scraps. The book is divided into five chapters, with items to wear on your head, around your neck, on your lapel or dangling from your ears, and also things to carry with you on your travels. You can, of course, personalize any of these items by choosing your own combinations of colours and patterns, perhaps to match an outfit exactly or to add a splash of colour to a plain ensemble. Most of the projects would also make delightful gifts for friends and family. I hope you enjoy making them.

Susie

THE BASICS

MATERIALS & EQUIPMENT

If you are keen on sewing, you will no doubt have most of the tools and equipment needed to complete the projects. All you will have to buy are some fat quarters of fabrics. For some of the jewellery items, you may need additional tools and components.

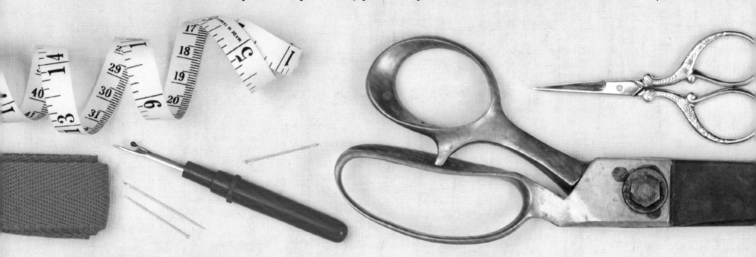

MEASURING Use either metric or imperial measurements: both are included in the pattern instructions, but do not mix the two.

You will need a long ruler for drawing lines on fabric, as well as a tape measure. A set square, right-angled ruler or quilter's square help to measure and mark out neat corners. Other useful measuring devices are available, such as gauges for marking evenly spaced lines (see Bag Tassel, page 116) and for helping to ensure neatly turned hems.

SCISSORS You will need dressmaking scissors for cutting fabrics and small, pointed embroidery scissors for snipping threads. Pinking shears are useful for trimming raw edges on seams, to prevent fraying; they can also be used for cutting decorative shapes from felt. Use a separate pair of scissors for cutting paper, as paper tends to blunt the blades. A rotary cutter, consisting of a sharp-edged round blade with a handle and a safety guard for when it's not in use, is a very useful tool when you need to produce accurate shapes or cut

through several layers of fabric at once. It should be used in conjunction with a special mat with a self-healing surface.

IRON A good steam iron is an essential piece of equipment. Make sure that your ironing board is firm and stable, with a well-padded surface. Press fabrics before measuring and cutting, then press the work regularly when sewing, for a neat finish. When pressing embroidery, place the work right side down on a folded towel and press on the reverse. The towel cushions the fabric and helps to prevent the embroidery stitches from being flattened.

SEAM RIPPER This tool is useful for cutting individual stitches and unpicking seams without damaging the fabric. Insert the pointed blade underneath the stitch to be cut, then push it forward against the thread.

PINS Before stitching, it is advisable to pin and tack layers of fabric together to prevent them from slipping when stitching by hand or machine. Pins

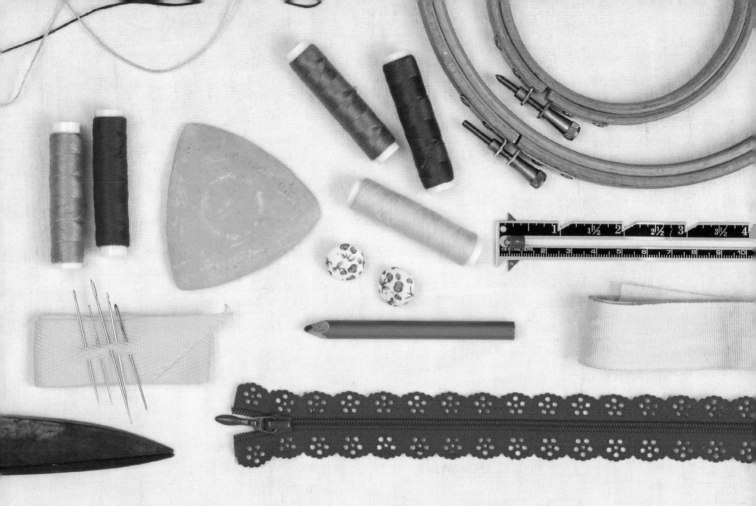

with glass heads are easy to handle and to find. Sometimes, however, pins distort the fabric or are difficult to use when there are lots of layers or tough fabrics, in which case you may find it easier to use binding clips. Safety pins can sometimes be used in place of straight pins to hold fabric layers together; they are also useful for threading elastic and cords through casings.

NEEDLES Sharps are an all-rounder for hand sewing, with a round eye that is easy to thread. For embroidery, an embroidery (crewel) needle has a longer eye, to accommodate thicker thread. For really thick thread, a chenille needle is larger, thicker and more robust. A bodkin or tapestry needle, having a large, long eye and a blunt tip, is useful for threading cords, thick threads and lengths of elastic through casings.

THREADS Use cotton thread when sewing cotton fabrics. It is available in a wide range of colours. Choose a thread to match the fabric as closely as possible, choosing a shade darker if you cannot

find an exact match. For quilting and gathering, you can use a slightly stronger thread.

For decorative stitching, embroidery thread is more substantial than ordinary sewing thread. Some projects call for six-stranded embroidery thread, which can be divided into individual strands, while some use perle cotton, which is a thicker, twisted thread.

For threading beads, use a strong nylon beading thread, or raid the bathroom cabinet for dental floss, which is firm and strong, ideal for the purpose.

EMBROIDERY HOOP For most types of embroidery, it is advisable to place the fabric to be stitched in an embroidery hoop, which holds it taut while you sew.

BOBBINS Keep a small stock of sewing-machine bobbins loaded with different-coloured threads, ready for use. When combining different-coloured fabrics, it can be useful to use one colour as a top thread and another on the bobbin.

JEWELLERY TOOLS

You will need a few basic tools to cut, bend and otherwise manipulate some of the metal components – known as findings – needed to complete some of the projects.

A pair of round-nosed pliers is essential for curling wire into neat, round loops, while the flat-nosed version is the right tool for opening jump rings and squashing things together. Some pliers also incorporate a wire cutter, but for those that don't a pair of wire snippers is also useful. For setting eyelets, you may need to use a hammer: a small, fairly lightweight one should be adequate. Some eyelets need a setting tool, while others require special pliers; check which you need when purchasing eyelets.

JEWELLERY FINDINGS

'Findings' are small components, usually made from metal, that are essential for making most types of earrings, necklaces, bracelets and other types of jewellery. There are thousands of different findings, a small selection of which have been used to create some of the projects on this book.

EAR WIRES

The style of earring fitting used in this book is a fish hook or French hook, suitable for pierced ears; other types are also available. If your ears are not pierced, there are various types of clip-on earrings available.

CLASPS

There are different types available and they are usually used to fasten necklaces that are too short to fit over the head. They can also be used for bracelets and other items. The various types include hooks, toggles, lobster clasps and bolt rings.

CHAINS

Linked chains can be bought by the yard or metre and cut to the desired length. Ball chains can also be bought like this and are also available with clasps attached, like the one used for the Luggage Label on page 128.

JUMP RINGS

These are used mainly to connect two components together. There are different sizes and thicknesses available. A jump ring needs to be opened and closed with a pair of pliers: hold the jump ring between your finger and thumb and grasp it with the pliers close to the gap, then push the metal to one side. Slip it through the piece you are joining, then push it back so that the two ends of the ring meet once more. When opening a jump ring, it is important to push it to one side and not pull the two ends apart, otherwise it will be difficult to re-close the gap. A split ring is sometimes used in place of a jump ring. This is slightly sturdier and less likely to be pulled apart in use, but it is more tricky to attach.

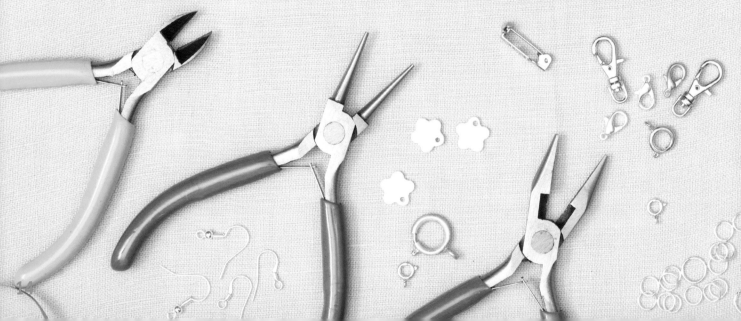

HEADPINS

A headpin is a pre-cut length of wire with a stopper, like the head of a pin, at one end, to prevent a bead from slipping off. An eyepin is similar, but has a loop at one end instead of a head, to allow you to attach a ring or charm. You can buy them ready-made or make your own by curling a loop at the end of a short length of wire, as in the Tassel Earrings, page 90.

SPACER BEADS

These are beads, often made from metal or glass, designed to fit inconspicuously between fancy beads, to space them out.

RIBBON END CRIMPS

These are available in a variety of lengths to fit different widths of ribbon. You simply insert the end of the ribbon, tape or braid into the crimp and squeeze the two sides together using flat-nosed pliers. The teeth on the crimp grip the fabric, holding it securely in place, and there is a small loop into which you can insert a jump ring to attach a clasp, chain or other findings.

WIRE

Jewellery wire is available in various thicknesses, or 'gauges'. A 0.6mm gauge is a good standard thickness, easy to bend yet reasonably strong. It is usually available to purchase in a roll from which you cut off the length you require, using wire cutters.

FABRICS

Medium-weight cotton fabrics are widely available as pre-cut fat quarters: these have been used throughout the book as the main fabrics. Where felt is used, craft felt is suitable for most items of jewellery but do bear in mind that craft felt will fall apart when it is washed, so you may prefer to buy felt made from wool or a wool blend, and ask when buying if it is washable. If you are unsure, wash a sample in the washing machine before using it in a project that might need to be laundered.

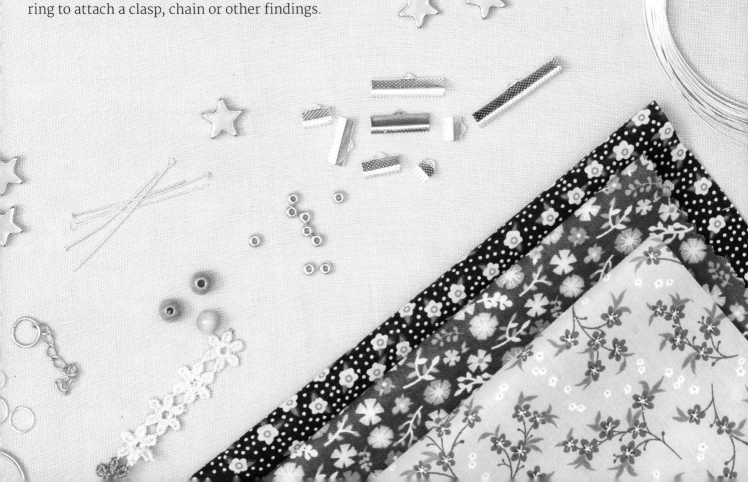

TECHNIQUES

The majority of the projects in this book involve basic sewing techniques, both by hand and machine. In this section you will find some basic instructions and tips to help you achieve a neat and professional-looking result.

PREPARING TO SEW

Preparation is important when embarking on any new project – and before you start sewing, there are a number of things you will need to do first.

MARKING FABRIC

When a project is made up of squares, rectangles and strips of fabric, measurements are given within the pattern instructions. You will need to measure and mark out these shapes on your fabric, using a ruler or a set square. Complex pattern pieces are printed at the back of the book, as templates. These need to be traced; or if they need to be enlarged, you can photocopy them.

Embroidery motifs can be traced directly onto fabric, especially if the fabric is light in colour. Just lay the fabric on top of the motif and trace over it. If it is difficult to see the lines of the design, you may need to use a light box – or photocopy or trace the motif onto plain paper and tape it onto a window, then place the fabric on top.

For drawing on fabric, use tailor's chalk or a chalk pencil, which can be rubbed away afterwards. Alternatively, you could use a water-erasable marker pen. An ordinary pencil or ballpoint pen can be used where the marks will be hidden in the seams or on the inside of the finished item, and also for drawing out designs to be embroidered when the lines will be completely hidden by the stitches.

INTERFACING, LININGS AND STABILIZERS

To add substance and sometimes stiffness to cotton fabrics, other materials are applied to the fabric pieces before they are assembled. The type and weight you need will be specified in the project. Fusible interfacing is a non-woven material that stiffens the fabric; it is available in three weights: light, medium and heavy. Fusible fleece is a soft, felted fabric that adds a little thickness and softness. Wadding (batting) – used for making quilts – also creates extra padding.

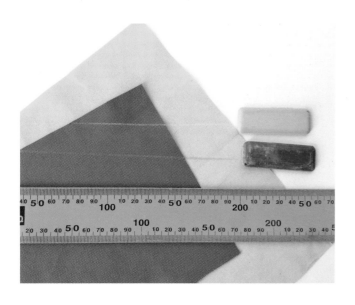

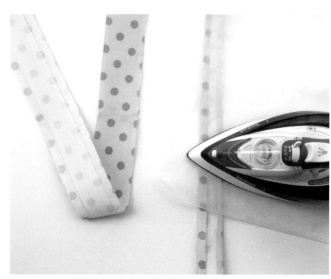

When using fusible materials, identify which side of the material is adhesive and place this side face down on the wrong side of the fabric. Place a piece of non-stick baking parchment on top, to protect the sole plate of the iron. You may also wish to place some scrap fabric between the fabric and the surface of the ironing board. Press with the iron set to hot or medium heat, whichever is recommended by the manufacturer. The heat will melt the adhesive and bond the interfacing or other material to the fabric. Try not to glide the iron, as this may cause the layers of fabric and interfacing to shift.

HAND SEWING

Sometimes you need to sew by hand, with needle and thread, prior to or instead of, machine sewing.

TACKING (BASTING)

Tacking is used to join layers of fabric together prior to sewing. Use a long running stitch for tacking. Running stitch is also used for gathering stitches. Start and finish with a couple of stitches worked over each other to secure the end of the thread, and work the stitches within the seam allowance.

SLIPSTITCH

When making items such as cushion covers or objects to be stuffed, you will need to join pieces with right sides together, leave a gap for turning that then has to be closed on the right side. Use slipstitch for this, for a neat and barely visible result. Fold in the raw edges on each side of the gap, then secure the thread in the end of the seam. Use the tip of the needle to pick up a small section of fabric along the fold on one side. Then pick up a small amount of fabric on the other side. Pull the thread to close the gap. Repeat all along the opening and fasten off.

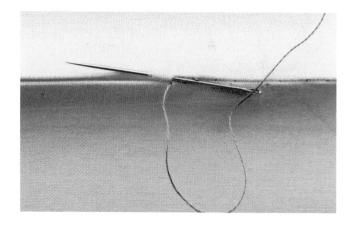

OVERSEWING

This technique, sometimes called whipstitch, is, like slipstitch, used to join two edges. These could be cut edges or folded edges. The stitches will be visible, so keep them small and neat. Line up the two edges and secure the end of the thread, then take the tip of the needle through one piece of fabric and then the other, usually from back to front, to make a small stitch. Repeat the process, always taking the needle through the fabric in the same direction.

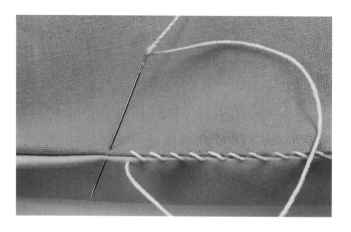

EMBROIDERY

CHAIN STITCH

This looped stitch can be worked along a curved or straight line. Bring the needle up through the fabric at the starting point. Insert the needle again in the same place, then bring the tip up through the fabric a short distance away. Loop the working thread around the tip of the needle and pull it through the loop. Re-insert the needle in the same place, just inside the loop, and repeat the process to make a line of linked stitches that form a chain. At the end of the line, make a small, straight stitch to anchor the final loop in place.

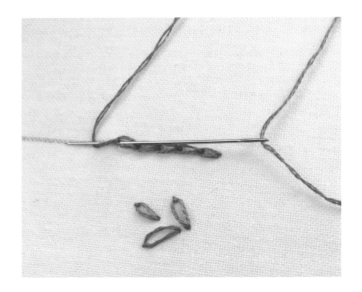

BLANKET STITCH

Blanket stitch is used to edge blankets; it can also be used to attach appliqué shapes to a background fabric. Buttonhole stitch is the same, the difference being that stitches are worked close together.

Start with the needle at the top edge of the fabric or just outside the edge of an appliqué shape and bring it back out directly below. This creates a small loop at the top. Take the needle up through the loop and pull to tighten the stitch; the vertical thread is now held in place by a small horizontal bar that runs along the edge of the fabric or the appliqué shape. You can choose the height of the stitch as you insert the needle and you can also alter the space between stitches.

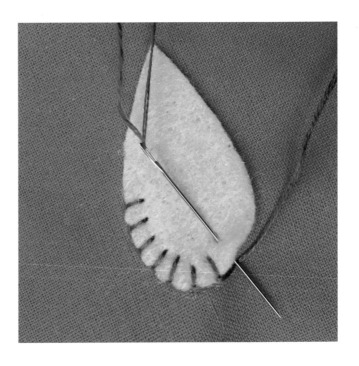

SATIN STITCH

This is suitable for filling small areas of a design. Work straight, parallel stitches close together to cover the shape to be filled. There should be no gaps between stitches. Try to keep the edges smooth and taut to ensure that all your stitches lie flat.

BACKSTITCH

Backstitch can be used to describe straight lines, wavy lines and curves. It is useful for outlining the edge of a shape and looks good in combination with most other embroidery stitches.

Working from right to left, bring the needle up through the fabric a little to the left of the beginning of the line to be worked, then back through at the beginning of the line and up again a stitch length in front of the place the needle first emerged. Repeat the process, going back in again at the starting point, then forward, a stitch length in front.

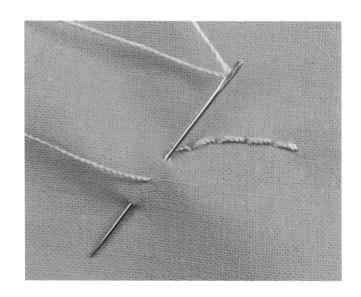

STEM STITCH

As the name implies, this stitch is useful for embroidering stems. It also makes a solid outline.

Working from left to right, bring the needle up at the beginning of the line to be worked, then down a stitch length to the right. Pull the thread through to form the first stitch. Bring the needle up just above the centre of the first stitch and along the line, to the right, another stitch length. Repeat the process along the length of the line. You can vary the length of the stitches and the slant, to make a thinner or thicker line.

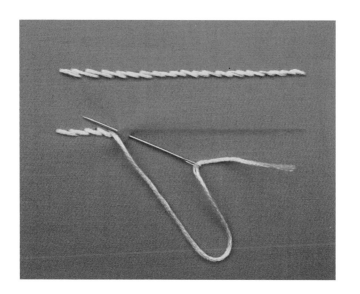

MACHINE SEWING

Most of the projects in this book are made using a sewing machine and straight stitch seams, to ensure that components are firmly joined together. Use the right size needle for the fabric – size 80 for medium-weight cotton – and change it frequently to ensure that the needle is sharp.

SETTING UP

Place the machine where there is plenty of light and you can sit comfortably. Make sure that the machine is threaded correctly and that the threads from the needle and the bobbin are placed away from you, towards the back of the base plate. When you start to stitch, turn the hand wheel to lower the needle into the fabric; this will help to prevent the threads from tangling. Before stitching your project, test the machine-stitch size and tension on a scrap of the fabric you are working with, and adjust if necessary.

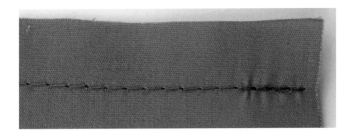

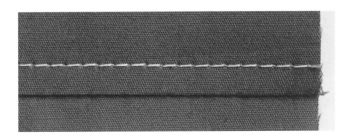

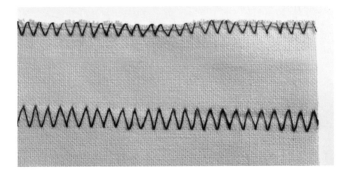

STRAIGHT STITCH

This is used for flat seams and topstitching, and for hemming. You can alter the length of the stitch, using a long stitch for tacking (basting) and gathering, for example. At the start and end of a line of stitching, backstitch for a few stitches. This will prevent the stitches from coming undone and you can snip off the threads close to the surface of the fabric.

TOPSTITCHING

Topstitching creates a crisp finish and holds layers of fabric neatly and securely in place. Press the seam to one side. Topstitch parallel to the seamline; the distance from the line is variable, but on a seam it will be a smaller measurement than the seam allowance to ensure that the raw edges of the fabric are trapped under the topstitching.

ZIGZAG STITCH

To attach appliqué shapes using a sewing machine, use a close zigzag stitch all around the edges to attach the shape to the fabric and prevent raw edges from fraying.

ADDITIONAL TECHNIQUES

BINDING EDGES

Here are two techniques for neatly covering raw edges with a long strip of fabric.

ONE-STEP BINDING

This method works best on a straight edge of firm fabric. Fold the binding in half down its length and press. Place the folded binding over the edge of the fabric, to enclose it completely. Pin and tack (baste) in place, then stitch close to the lower edge of the binding, checking on the other side that the stitching has captured both long edges.

TWO-STEP BINDING

When binding an uneven edge, a corner or curve, two-step binding is the preferred method.

1 Open out the binding and line up one raw edge of the binding with the edge of the fabric. Pin and tack to hold in place, then stitch along the foldline by hand or machine.

2 Fold the binding over to enclose the raw edges, and slipstitch the other long folded edge of the binding on the seamline.

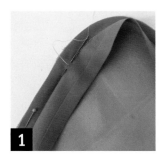
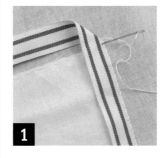

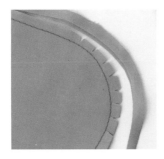

CLIPPING AND TURNING

Corners should be cut across at an angle so that they are sharp when the work is turned right side out. On curved seams, cut 'V' shapes into the seam allowance, close to the stitchline. Snip very carefully with small, sharp scissors to avoid cutting through the stitches by mistake. When turning items right side out, a corner and edge shaper, which is a flattish shape with one rounded and one pointed but slightly blunt end, is useful, as the name implies, for pushing out the corners and edges for a neat finish.

MITRED CORNER

This technique has been used to create a frame from ribbon on the Pendant (see page 32). It is also a neat way of finishing a bound edge, in which case you will need to make two 45-degree folds, one on each side of the fabric – but the principle is the same.

1 Pin and stitch the outer edge of the ribbon or braid about half the ribbon's width beyond the corner to be covered. Fold the ribbon under, making the fold at a 45-degree angle, so the ribbon now follows the adjacent edge.

2 Bring the ribbon down, so it straddles the raw edge of the fabric and the 45-degree fold forms a neat corner. Stitch the outer edge in place, as before, followed by the inner edge. You may wish to make a few small, neat stitches on the folded corner itself.

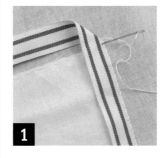
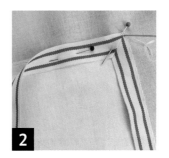

LOOP TURNER

Making a narrow tube of fabric can be fiddly, but the task is easier if you use a loop turner, sometimes called a rouleau turner, which is a long metal pin with a ring on one end and a clip on the other. Insert the loop turner into the tube of fabric and attach the clip to the end of the seam, then pull the loop turner back through the tube.

NECKWEAR

TASSELLED PATCHWORK SCARF

Here, a simple patchwork scarf is given an unusual twist with the addition of hand-made tassels: it's the perfect finishing touch for any occasion, formal or informal. You'll need eight different fabrics – which gives you a great excuse to visit your local quilting store and play around with different combinations of colour and pattern.

You will need
8 fat quarters of printed cotton fabric,
    all different
2¼yd (2m) length of narrow ribbon or tape
Sewing thread to match fabric
Ruler
Dressmaker's chalk pencil
Pins
Dressmaking scissors
Sewing needle
Sewing machine (optional)
Iron and ironing board

NOTE:
When joining the patchwork pieces, the squares of fabric are offset, which not only looks attractive but dispenses with the need to carefully line up the seams. This means that making the scarf is relatively quick and easy to do.

Finished size is roughly:
64 x 10in (162 x 25cm)

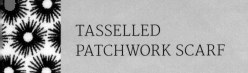

1 Using a ruler and a dressmaker's chalk pencil, mark out and cut 12 squares measuring 4¾in (12cm) from each of the eight fat quarters.

Tip

You may prefer to use a rotary cutter and self-healing cutting mat to cut out the patchwork squares. The advantage of this method is that it is very accurate and you can cut several layers of fabric at once.

2 Stitch 16 squares together with a ¼in (6mm) seam allowance, to make one long strip. The strip will comprise two squares of each pattern, pieced together in the same order. Press the seams open.

3 Make five more strips in the same way. Start each strip with a different print and follow the same order of squares as the first strip.

4 Stitch the strips together, again with a ¼in (6mm) seam allowance, offsetting them so that the seams on one strip are aligned with the centres of the squares on the adjacent strip. This not only dispenses with the need to align seams, but also distributes the bulk more evenly and produces an attractive design. Press each long seam open.

5 Trim the two short ends of the patchwork. Reserve each of the six half-squares: these will be used later, to make tassels.

6 Fold the patchwork in half lengthways, right sides together, and stitch the two long ends together with a ¼in (6mm) seam allowance, leaving a gap in the centre of the seam of approximately 6in (15cm). Flatten the fabric tube, placing the seam you have just sewn down the centre; press the seam open.

7 Cut 26 2¾in (7cm) lengths of ribbon or tape. Insert half of these into one end of the scarf, evenly spaced and with one cut end level with the raw edges of the fabric; do the same with the remaining lengths at the other end of the scarf. Pin each one in place, then stitch across the ends of the scarf with a ¼in (6mm) seam allowance, trapping the ribbons in the seam.

8 Turn the scarf right side out through the gap in the seam. Slipstitch (see page 17) the folded edges together to close the gap.

9 To make the tassels, cut 20 pieces of fabric each measuring 4¾ x 2½in (12 x 6cm); with the pieces trimmed off in step 5, you will have 26 small rectangles. Fold each one in half with right sides together, then stitch up both sides with a ¼in (6mm) seam allowance.

10 On the top edge of each tassel, turn ⅜in (1cm) to wrong side. Sew a running stitch (see page 17) along the fold on each one. Turn the tassels right side out. To attach each tassel, insert the end of the ribbon, pull up the running stitch to gather the top, and stitch firmly in place.

SCALLOP-EDGED COLLAR

This pretty patchwork collar is quick and easy to make and really brightens up a plain, round-necked dress, T-shirt or sweater. Each section of the collar is quite small, so it's perfect for using up scraps from your stash — but be sure to use small-scale prints.

Find the templates on pages 132-3

You will need
1 fat quarter of printed cotton fabric, for the backing
Scraps of 5 different printed cotton fabrics,
    at least 6 x 4in (15 x 10cm), for the patchwork
20in (50cm) cotton bias binding, ⅝in (1.5cm) wide
¾in (19mm) fabric-covered button (see steps 2-3, page 96)
3½in (9cm) length of cord elastic
Sewing thread to match fabric
Thin card or plastic, for templates
Dressmaker's chalk pencil
Sewing needle
Sewing machine (optional)
All-purpose scissors
Dressmaking scissors
Corner and edge shaper
Iron and ironing board
Pins

NOTE: Use thin card to cut templates. Sewing suppliers also sell sheets of rigid plastic, which is easy to cut with scissors and longer lasting than card, so this is ideal if you are making a number of items from one pattern.

Finished size:
Width at widest point: 5in (12.5cm)
Fits most neck sizes

1 Make patterns from card or plastic for the different pieces of the collar, using the templates on pages 132-3. Cut two of the large scalloped-edged pieces from the fat quarter: this will form the backing. The other templates are numbered 1 to 5: number 1 will be at the front of the collar and number 5 at the back. Mark and cut two of each numbered shape, placing or folding the fabric right sides together when cutting so that one piece will be a mirror image of the other.

2 To make the two halves of the collar, join the pieces in numbered order with a ¼in (6mm) seam allowance.

3 Iron both collar pieces, pressing all the seams open.

4 Pin the two patchwork pieces right sides together, aligning all the edges, and stitch together along the straight edge of piece 1 with a ⁵⁄₁₆in (8mm) seam allowance. This seam will be at the front of the collar. Repeat with the two backing pieces. Press the seams open.

Tip

The collar is made up from custom-shaped pieces joined together to make a patchwork, which is then lined with a single piece of fabric. This means it is important to join the patchwork pieces as accurately as possible, or they will not end up the same shape and size as the lining. If this happens, however, in step 6, when the lining is attached, simply trim the edges but make sure you trim the same amount from both sides of the collar, or it will be uneven.

5 Place the collar and backing right sides together, matching the edges, and pin.

6 Tack the two layers together all around the scalloped edge (see page 17). Trim the edges, if necessary.

7 Stitch the layers together all round the scalloped edge with a ¼in (6mm) seam allowance, leaving the neck edge unstitched. Snip into the seam allowance on all the curves (see page 21).

8 Turn the collar right side out through the opening on the neck edge. Use a corner and edge shaper, or similar blunt tool, to push out all the curved edges.

9 Open out the bias binding and align one long edge with the neck edge of the right side of the collar. Stitch along the opened-out foldline of the binding, through all layers, by hand or machine (see page 21).

10 Turn the collar over. Fold the cord elastic in half to form a loop, place the two ends on the right-hand corner of the collar, within the seam allowance, and stitch them firmly to the fabric.

11 Fold the bias binding over the neck edge of the collar, covering the ends of the elastic as you do so, and pin the binding in place, then slipstitch the folded edge to the fabric (see page 17). When you have done this, sew a fabric-covered button to the corner opposite the elastic loop.

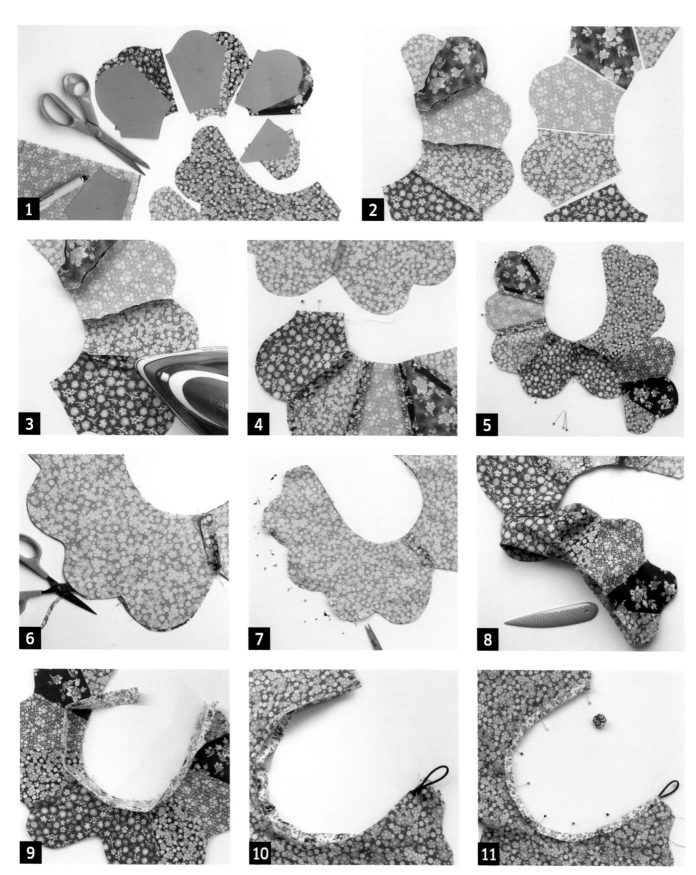

PENDANT

Show off your talent for embroidery with this floral pendant. It makes good use of leftover fabric, ribbon and braid from your workbasket. Choose a subtle print as the background for the embroidery and co-ordinating prints for the backing and the neck strap. There's also an optional secret pocket on the back.

Find the template on page 134

Finished size is roughly:
Pendant is approx. 4³/₈ x 4in (11 x 10cm), excluding charms; straps are 15in (38cm) long.

You will need
Cotton print fabric, approximately 6in (15cm) square
Contrast fabric, approximately 11 x 5in (28 x 12.5cm)
Contrast fabric, 4in (10cm) square, for the pocket (optional)
16in (40cm) length of three different ribbons or braids, each approximately ³/₈in (8–10mm) wide
12in (30cm) length of fine silk ribbon, ³/₁₆in (4mm) wide
Six-stranded embroidery thread (floss) in coral pink and pale green, or your own choice of colours
Sewing thread to match fabric
Glass seed beads, approximately two dozen
5 jump rings, ⁵/₁₆in (7mm) diameter
2 ribbon end crimps, ³/₈in (1cm)
5 flower-shaped charms
Flower-shaped buttons (optional)
Lobster claw clasp and jump ring fastening (or similar)
Water-soluble fabric marker pen
Permanent fabric marker pen or pencil
Dressmaking scissors
5in (12.5cm) embroidery hoop
Crewel needle
Sewing needle
Fine sewing needle or beading needle
Flat-nosed pliers
Iron and ironing board

NOTE: The crimp at the end of the strap has a little loop built in, which makes it simple to attach a clasp securely.

1 Trace or photocopy the flower motif from page 134 onto plain paper, then trace it onto the centre of the fabric square, using a water-soluble marker for the flower design and a permanent pen or pencil for the outline.

2 Place the fabric in an embroidery hoop and, using two strands of coral pink embroidery thread (floss), fill in the flower petals in satin stitch (see page 18).

3 Embroider the leaves in satin stitch and the stems in stem stitch (see page 19), using two strands of green thread. Sew a glass seed bead in place on each small dot on the design, using a fine sewing needle or beading needle and a single strand of thread.

4 Wash out the design lines using cold water and leave to dry, then press lightly on the reverse. Trim the embroidered fabric along the lines you have drawn.

5 Cut two pieces of contrasting fabric, each measuring 5¼ x 4¾in (13 x 12cm). Put one aside, for the backing. Place the embroidery in the centre of the other one and stitch it in place all round.

6 Create a border: start by stitching a length of ribbon in place, lining up the straight edge of the tape with the edge of the embroidered fabric panel and creating a mitre at each corner (see page 21). Then sew a second, contrasting length of ribbon in place, aligning the edges. Sew fancy braid on top, covering the join between the two ribbons.

7 Cut the fine ribbon into five equal lengths, slip a jump ring onto each one and tie a single knot in the centre to hold the jump ring in place. Pin each one in place, evenly spaced, lining up the edge of each ring with the edge of the ribbon border, then stitch to the lower edge of the fabric.

8 Make the neck straps. To do this, cut two strips of fabric each 15 x 1½in (38 x 4cm). Fold each one in half lengthways, with right sides together, and stitch with a ⅜in (1cm) seam allowance. Turn right side out, press, and attach a ⅜in (1cm) ribbon end crimp to one end of each, using flat-nosed pliers to close the crimp (see page 15).

9 Pin and stitch the raw end of each strap to the top of the pendant, with the edge of each strap ⅜in (1cm) in from the edge on each side.

10 Fold ⅜in (1cm) to the wrong side on all four edges. Do the same with the reserved piece of fabric. If you want to add any further embellishment to the front – such as a button or two to cover an untidy join on the bottom corner of the border – or if you want to add a pocket to the back, now is the time to do it, before the front and back are joined.

11 To make a secret pocket, cut a piece of fabric measuring 4in (10cm) square, fold in and press ⅜in (1cm) to the wrong side on all four edges. Topstitch (see page 20) one edge: this will be the opening at the top. Place centrally on the backing and stitch in place on both sides and across the bottom. Place the front and back of the pendant wrong sides together and oversew (see page 17) the edges together all round.

12 Using pliers, attach a charm to each of the jump rings along the bottom. Attach a jump ring to the end of one strap and a lobster claw clasp to the other (see page 14).

MULTI-STRAND NECKLACE

Inspired by tribal jewellery, this chunky necklace makes a dramatic fashion statement. Be as bold as you dare with your colour combinations – this is a flamboyant, eye-catching piece that demands to be noticed.

You will need
Fat quarters of fabric, various prints
Chunky knitting yarn
Perle cotton thread
Round wooden beads, $\frac{3}{8}$in (9mm) diameter
1 button, $\frac{3}{4}$in (2cm) diameter
Sewing thread to match fabric
Six-stranded embroidery thread (floss) in one or two colours
Ruler
Dressmaker's chalk pencil
Dressmaking scissors
Sewing needle or sewing machine
Loop turner
Bodkin or blunt tapestry needle
Crewel needle
Chenille needle
Iron and ironing board

NOTE: Wooden beads are lightweight, so the finished necklace won't be too heavy. You will need 25–30 beads for a single strand, or maybe a few more, depending on what size they are and how far apart you space them.

Finished size is roughly:
27½in (70cm) long

1 Mark and cut out strips measuring 21 x 1½in (54 x 4cm) for plain strands and 21 x 2in (54 x 5cm) for beaded strands. The necklace shown here comprises eight plain strands and two beaded strands – but you may prefer to have fewer or more strands for your necklace.

2 Fold each strip in half lengthways, right sides together, and stitch down the length with a ¼in (6mm) seam allowance. Trim the seam allowance to reduce bulk and turn each strip right side out. A loop turner (see page 21) is useful for this.

3 To make the plain strands more substantial and rounded, you will need to pad them out. To do this, cut a length of chunky knitting yarn approximately two and a half times the length of the fabric tube and thread it onto a bodkin or blunt tapestry needle, so that the bodkin is positioned halfway along its length. Push the bodkin through the tube of fabric until it emerges at the other end. Cut the yarn, leaving a little protruding from each end of the tube. Repeat until you have the required number of strands.

4 To make a beaded strand, cut a length of perle cotton thread about twice the length of the fabric strip, thread it into a crewel or chenille needle and attach it to one end of one of the wider fabric tubes. Insert a bead into the tube and push the needle into the fabric just below the bead, through the hole in the centre of the bead and out the other side. Wind the thread around the fabric and tie it in a tight knot, then add another bead and repeat the process. Continue until the fabric tube has been filled.

5 Lay the strands flat and arrange them until you are happy with the result.

6 Thread the chenille needle with a length of perle cotton thread and take it through each of the strands in turn. Trim off the excess chunky yarn, then pull up the thread to push the strand ends close together and fasten off.

7 Repeat step 6 at the other end of the necklace. You will need to trim off more from some of the strands, depending on their position in the arrangement.

8 For the neck straps, cut two pieces of fabric each 10 x 4½in (25 x 12cm). Stitch the top ends of the strands to the straps with a ½in (12mm) seam allowance.

9 Fold back the strap pieces and press. At the top edge of each, fold ½in (12mm) to the wrong side and press. On one long edge, fold ¾in (2cm) to the wrong side and on the other long edge fold 1½in (4cm) to the wrong side; press.

10 Fold in all the pressed edges. There should be a fold down the centre of the strap: slipstitch this in place (see page 17), using thread to match the fabric.

11 Cut a ¾in (2cm) vertical slit near the end of one strap and sew around it with close buttonhole stitch (see page 18), using a crewel needle and a single strand of embroidery thread (floss) to match the fabric. Stitch a button on the other strap, to correspond with the buttonhole.

12 As a finishing touch, sew lines of running stitch, equally spaced, along the length of each strap, using two strands of embroidery thread in a contrast colour.

ROLLED BEAD NECKLACE

If you're keen on recycling and avoiding waste, this is another of those projects that utilizes small scraps. The rolled beads are hand made from strips of colourful fabrics (small-scale tie-dye and batik-style prints work particularly well) interspersed with simple wooden beads, for a boho chic look that's never out of fashion.

You will need
Scraps of printed cotton fabric at least
    4³/4 x 2¹/2in (12 x 6cm)
Medium-weight non-fusible interfacing,
    at least 13 x 6in (32 x 15cm)
20 round wooden beads, ³/8in (9mm) diameter
40 wooden disc beads, ¹/4in (6mm) diameter
Six-stranded embroidery thread (floss) in various colours
Sewing thread to match fabric
Strong nylon beading thread
Ruler
Dressmaker's chalk pencil
Dressmaking scissors or rotary cutter and cutting mat
Small knitting needle (approx. 4mm/US 6)
Crewel needle
Beading needle
Iron and ironing board
Binding clip (optional)
All-purpose glue

Finished size is roughly:
36in (90cm) long. (This length may vary slightly from the measurement given, depending on the finished length of the rolled beads and the diameter of the wooden beads you use. If you want a longer necklace, simply make a few more beads.)

1 From various different fabrics, cut 20 pieces each measuring 4³⁄₄ x 2¹⁄₂in (12 x 6cm) and 20 pieces measuring 4¹⁄₄ x 1¹⁄₄in (11 x 3cm). From interfacing, cut 20 pieces measuring 3 x 1¹⁄₄in (8 x 3cm).

2 On each fabric strip, large and small, turn ¹⁄₄in (6mm) to the wrong side on one of the short ends and press. Then bring the two long edges to meet at the centre and press. The edges do not have to be exactly in the centre of the strip, but they should meet and not overlap.

3 Insert a piece of interfacing about halfway into the unfolded end of each of the larger fabric pieces. Fix in place with a few hand stitches, taking the needle through all the layers.

4 Now insert the unfolded end of a smaller piece of fabric into the folded end of each larger piece. Mix and match the patterns and colours. Tack (baste) through all the layers (see page 17).

5 Starting with the interfacing, start to roll the strip tightly around the knitting needle.

6 Continue rolling until you reach the end of the larger fabric piece.

7 Thread a crewel needle with two strands of embroidery thread (floss): you can use either a contrasting or a co-ordinating colour. Oversew (see page 17) the edges of the fabric roll, taking the needle through all layers.

8 Continue rolling the strip until it is completely wound. Using a single strand of sewing thread, slipstitch (see page 17) the edge of the smaller strip to the bead.

9 Using two strands of embroidery thread, sew several decorative lines of running stitch at intervals all around each bead.

10 Cut two lengths of strong beading thread, each approximately 60in (1.5m) long. Thread them into a beading needle and thread on one small disc bead followed by a round wooden bead, then another disc bead. Place a binding clip at one end of the strands of thread, if you wish, to prevent the beads from falling off.

11 Thread a fabric bead onto the thread, followed by another trio of wooden beads. Continue until you have used up all the beads, or until your necklace is the desired length.

12 Knot the ends of the threads together and put a small spot of glue on the knot to make it secure. Leave the glue to dry, then trim off the ends of the thread close to the knot.

HEADWEAR

SUN HAT

Pretty as well as practical, this wide-brimmed hat will keep you cool on even the hottest of days. As it's made from a lightweight cotton fabric, you can fold it up and tuck it into a pocket or handbag, ready to wear when the sun comes out.

Find the templates on pages 136-7

You will need
2 fat quarters of the same printed cotton fabric, for the brim
1 fat quarter of cotton fabric in a contrast print, for the crown
1 fat quarter of plain cotton fabric, for the lining
Heavyweight fusible interfacing, at least 20in (50cm) square
Sewing thread to match main fabric and lining
¾yd (70cm) length of cotton bias binding, ¾in (2cm) wide,
   to match or co-ordinate with lining fabric
Card for making pattern pieces
Dressmaker's chalk pencil
Pins
Dressmaking scissors
Sewing needle
Sewing machine
Iron and ironing board

NOTE: Take care to sew accurate seams so that the crown and brim fit together well. If your seams are too skimpy and the finished hat is a little too large, stitch a length of petersham ribbon all round, inside the crown, oversewing one long edge to the seamline; this will help to ensure a snug fit.

Finished size:
The hat is in one size, to fit a head circumference of approximately 22–23in (56–58.5cm)

1 Cut patterns for the different sections of the hat from card, using the templates on pages 136-7. Place the two fat quarters of fabric for the brim right sides together. Draw around the outline of the patterns, using a dressmaker's chalk pencil, and cut four brim pieces, ensuring that the straight edge that will form the centre back seam follows the straight grain of the fabric. Cut two crown sides from contrast and lining fabric, and one crown centre from contrast and lining fabric.

2 Pin each pair of brim pieces right sides together. Join the centre back seam on each pair of brim pieces with a $\frac{1}{4}$in (6mm) seam allowance. Press the seams open.

3 Using one of the joined brim pieces as a template, cut one piece of heavyweight fusible interfacing. Trim off $\frac{1}{8}$in (2–3mm) all round the interfacing, then place it glue side down on the wrong side of the brim piece and fuse in place with a hot iron.

4 Join the front seam on each brim piece with a $\frac{1}{4}$in (6mm) seam allowance. Press the seams open.

5 Place the two brim pieces right sides together, matching the front and back seams. Stitch them together all round the outer edge with a $\frac{1}{4}$in (6mm) seam allowance. Snip into the seam allowance all round (see page 21).

6 Turn right side out through the centre and press. Topstitch (see page 20) all round $\frac{3}{8}$in (1cm) from the outer edge. Stitch concentric lines of topstitching $\frac{3}{8}$in (1cm) apart until you reach a point approximately $\frac{3}{8}$in (1cm) from the inner edge (see tip).

Tip

When topstitching the brim, start and end each round on the back seam. As you complete a round, don't cut the thread – swivel the work by 90°, sew $\frac{3}{8}$in (1cm) along the seamline, then swivel back and work the next round. This will help to ensure a neat finish without lots of thread ends to deal with.

7 Make the crown. Taking the pieces of contrast print fabric, place one side piece on either side of the central strip and, with right sides together and notches matched up, pin, tack (baste), and stitch together with a $\frac{1}{4}$in (6mm) seam allowance (see page 17). Repeat with the lining pieces. Snip into the curved edges and press the seams to one side, towards the central strip.

8 With wrong sides together, push the lining inside the crown, making sure that the seams and raw edges match. Tack the two layers together all round, close to the raw edges.

9 With right sides together, pin the crown to the brim. The centre strip of the crown, at either end, should align with the front and back seams on the brim. Stitch together with a $\frac{1}{4}$in (6mm) seam allowance.

10 Open out one long edge of the bias binding and line it up with the raw edges of the seam you have just stitched (see page 21). Backstitch (see page 19) along the fold. Then fold the binding over to cover the seam and slipstitch (see page 17) the folded edge to the seamline on the inside of the hat.

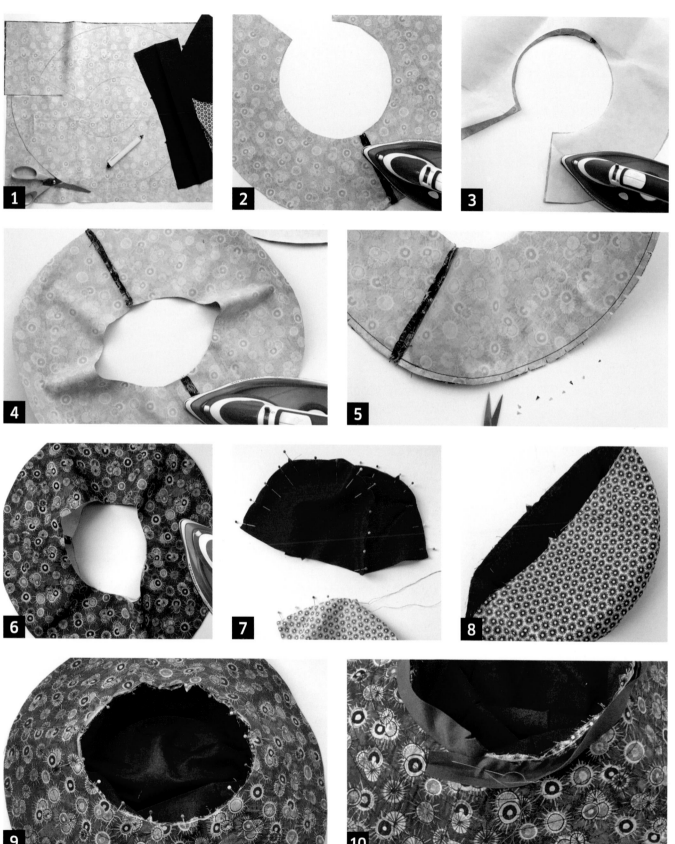

HEAD WRAP

Tired of your hair getting in the way while you're doing your make-up? Looking for a stylish accessory for those bad-hair days? This simple-to-stitch head wrap is just the thing! Why not make several in different fabric combinations?

You will need
2 fat quarters of printed cotton fabric
6in (15cm) length of elastic, 1¼in (3cm) wide
Sewing thread to match fabric
Pen or pencil
Ruler
Dressmaking scissors
Pins or binding clips
Sewing needle or sewing machine
Safety pin
Iron and ironing board

NOTE: This head wrap can be sewn by hand or by machine. Whichever you choose, make sure you sew very firm seams in steps 10 and 11, going over the stitching two or three times to hold the elastic securely in place.

Finished size:
To fit an adult's head

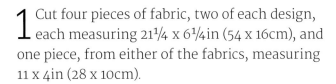

1 Cut four pieces of fabric, two of each design, each measuring 21¼ x 6¼in (54 x 16cm), and one piece, from either of the fabrics, measuring 11 x 4in (28 x 10cm).

2 Pair two pieces of fabric with different designs. With right sides together, pin or clip them together along both long edges, then stitch with a ⅜in (1cm) seam allowance, leaving the short ends unstitched. You now have two tubes of fabric. Press the seams open.

3 Turn both tubes right side out. Place the seams in the centre of each piece and press.

4 Place one strip centrally on top of the other, at right angles.

5 Align the two short edges on each piece and hold in place using pins or binding clips.

6 Make the elasticated back piece. Fold the remaining fabric rectangle in half lengthways and stitch the long edges together with a ⅜in (1cm) seam allowance. Trim the seam allowance to reduce bulk. Turn right side out.

7 Position the seam centrally on one side and press. Attach a safety pin to one end of the elastic.

8 Insert the elastic into the fabric, using the pin to guide it through. Stitch one end of the elastic to the end of the fabric. Continue pulling the pin through until the other end of the elastic emerges. Stitch this end of the elastic to the other end of the fabric.

9 On one end of the wrap, remove the clips and place the elasticated section inside, centring it over the seam and lining up the raw edges.

10 Fold the two sides over so that the elasticated piece is sandwiched between the other two fabric layers. Pin or clip, to hold the layers together, then stitch across, through all thicknesses, with a ⅜in (1cm) seam allowance.

11 Do the same with the other end of the wrap and the other end of the elasticated section. Trim the seam allowance or finish the raw edges by oversewing (see page 17), if you wish, bearing in mind that they will not be visible but will be hidden inside the folds of the head wrap.

12 Pull out the fabric so that the seams are hidden inside the folds.

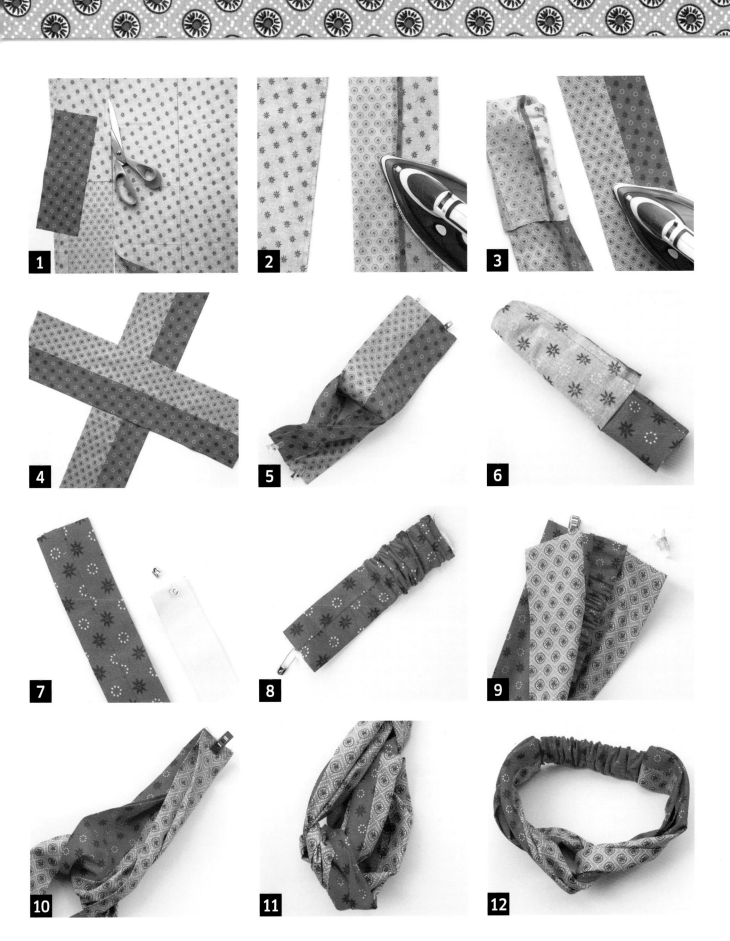

CLOCHE HAT

Although the style is associated with the Roaring Twenties — the age of speakeasies and flappers dancing the Charleston — this cloche hat is a timeless classic that's just perfect for a summer garden party or wedding. The pattern is given in two sizes to ensure a head-hugging fit.

Find the templates on pages 134-5

You will need
1 fat quarter of main printed cotton fabric, for the crown
1 fat quarter of contrast printed cotton fabric, for the brim
1 fat quarter of plain cotton fabric, for the lining
10in (25cm) medium-weight fusible interfacing
Sewing thread to match fabric
Pencil, dressmaker's chalk or fabric marker
Ruler
Paper for patterns
Pins
Dressmaking scissors
General-purpose scissors
Sewing machine
Sewing needle
Iron and ironing board

Finished size is roughly:
small fits heads 21¼–22in (54–56cm) and large fits heads 22¼–23in (56.5–58.5cm)

NOTE: The cloche pictured here is decorated with a fabric flower. To make it, you will need a remnant of the main fabric, a piece of lace and a self-covering button. You will find the quantities and instructions for making the flower on pages 62–65.

1 Cut two rectangles of main fabric, each 20½ x 7½in (52 x 19cm), measuring them along the length of the fat quarter. With right sides together, stitch the two pieces together along the short ends with a ³/₈in (1cm) seam allowance, matching the fabric pattern carefully as this seam will be at the centre front of the hat. Press the seam open.

2 Make paper patterns for the different sections of the hat, using the templates on pages 134–5. Using the side crown pattern piece, cut one from main fabric by folding the joined piece from step 1 right sides together along the seamline, placing the broken line on the pattern along this line, and cutting out through both layers.

3 Cut two rectangles, each 20½ x 6½in (52 x 16.5cm), from the contrast fabric. Stitch the two pieces together, as before, to make one long strip. Fold this along the seamline. Cut the brim from this fabric. Cut a side crown piece from the plain fabric, to form the lining, and a top crown piece from both the main fabric and the lining.

4 Use the same paper pattern pieces to cut one each of the three shapes from interfacing, then trim away ¹/₈in (3mm) all round.

NOTE: If you are buying interfacing by the yard (metre) from a roll, ¼yd (25cm) will be ample. For this project, you will need approximately 36 x 5½in (90 x 14cm).

5 Following the manufacturer's instructions, apply the interfacing to the wrong side of the top crown, side crown and brim (see page 17). Protect the sole plate of the iron by placing a piece of non-stick baking parchment between the iron and the interfacing.

6 Stitch the two short edges of the main fabric side crown together with a ³/₈in (1cm) seam allowance. Press the seam open.

7 With right sides together, pin and tack (baste) the main fabric top crown to the main fabric side crown (see page 17), matching the centre line to the front and back seams. Join the lining pieces in the same way.

8 With right sides together and a ³/₈in (1cm) seam allowance, stitch the centre back seam of the brim. Press the seam open.

9 Fold the brim in half lengthways, wrong sides together. Press, then tack the raw edges together.

10 With right sides together, matching front and back seams and aligning the raw edges, pin the brim to the crown, then stitch all round with a ³/₈in (1cm) seam allowance.

11 Turn under ³/₈in (1cm) all round the lower edge of the lining. Press.

12 To attach the lining, slipstitch (see page 17) the folded edge of the lining to the seamline on the hat, where the brim is attached to the crown. Push the lining inside the hat.

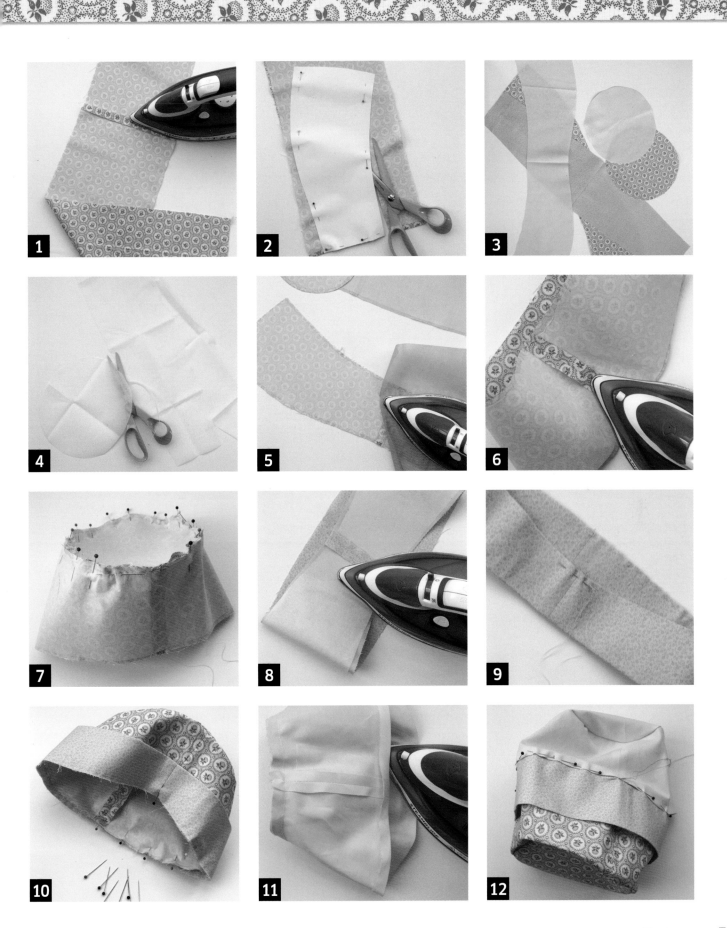

SCRUNCHIE

Anyone with long hair needs to tie it up from time to time. A scrunchie –
a ring of fabric-covered elastic – is ideal, as it will securely hold a ponytail or
bunches without damaging your hair. This one features the optional addition
of a bow, which adds a decorative flourish.

Find the template on page 138

You will need
1 fat quarter of printed cotton fabric
8in (20cm) length of elastic, ¼in (6mm) wide
Sewing thread to match fabric
Paper for making pattern
Pencil, dressmaker's chalk or fabric marker
Ruler
Safety pin or bodkin
Loop turner
Pins
Dressmaking scissors
General-purpose scissors
Sewing needle
Sewing machine (optional)
Iron and ironing board

NOTE: The instructions shown here are to make a scrunchie
with tails in the same fabric. You could, of course, make the
scrunchie in one fabric and the tails in a contrasting one.

Finished size is roughly:
*8½in (21.5cm) from end to
end of bow*

SCRUNCHIE

1 Mark out and cut a strip of fabric measuring 20 x 4in (50 x 10cm). Mark out and cut two tail pieces, using a paper pattern made from the template on page 138.

2 On one short end of the strip of fabric, fold ³⁄₈in (1cm) to the wrong side and press.

3 Fold the strip in half lengthways, right sides together, and sew along the long unfolded edge with a ³⁄₈in (1cm) seam allowance. Trim the seam allowance to reduce bulk.

4 Turn the fabric tube right side out with the help of a loop turner (see page 21). Press, placing the seam down the centre.

5 Attach one end of the elastic to a safety pin or bodkin. Use this to thread the elastic through the tube, making sure that the free end of the elastic does not get lost inside the fabric.

6 Overlap the ends of the elastic by ³⁄₈in (1cm) and stitch them together securely by hand or machine.

7 Insert the raw end of the tube into the folded end so that they overlap by about ³⁄₈in (1cm). Make sure the tube is not twisted. Slipstitch (see page 17) close to the fold to join the two ends of the tube together.

8 Place the two shaped bow pieces right sides together, and stitch all round, with a ¼in (6mm) seam allowance, leaving a gap of 4in (10cm) on one straight edge. Clip into the seam allowance on the curves (see page 21).

9 Turn right side out. Fold the seam allowance on the opening to the inside and slipstitch the folded edges together to close the gap.

10 Place the tail piece over the scrunchie and tie the ends in a single knot, which will cover the place where the two ends of the scrunchie are joined.

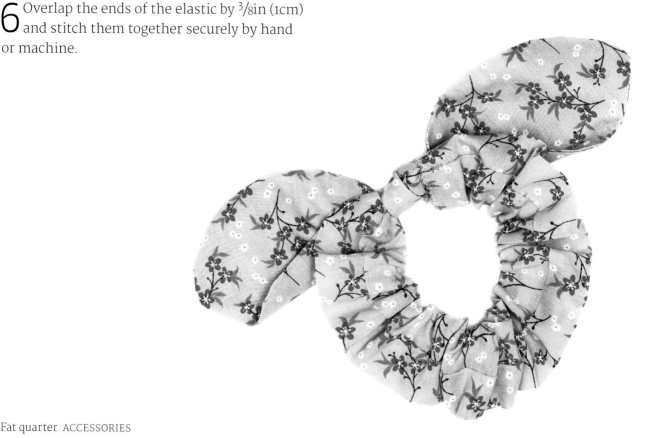

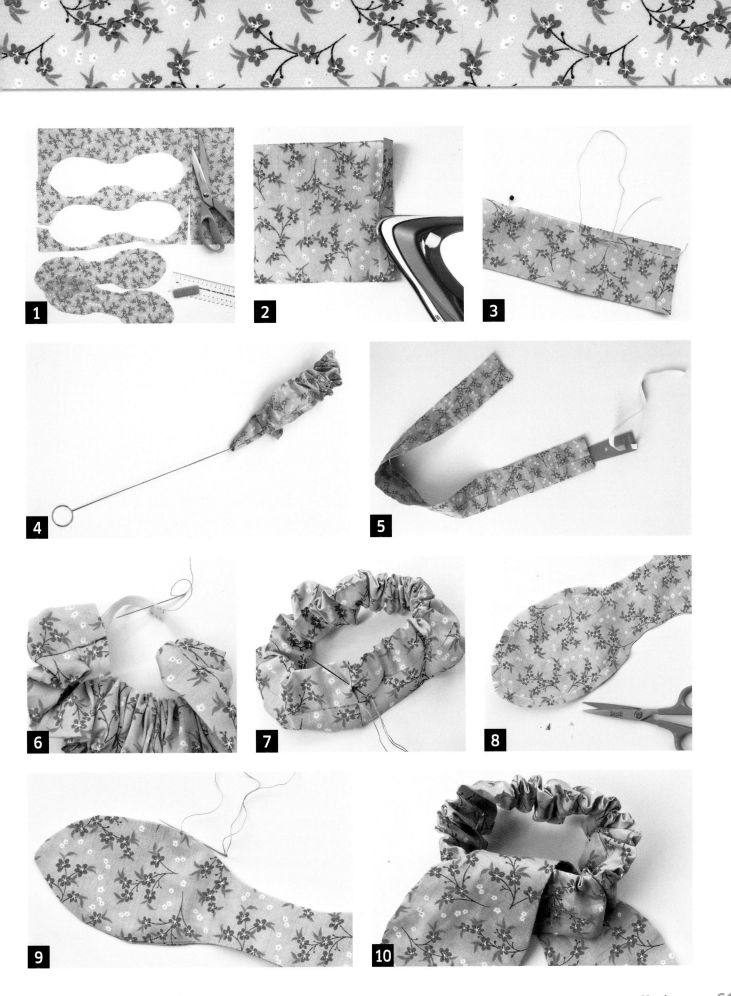

FASCINATOR

For special occasions such as weddings, a fascinator provides endless scope for creativity. This one features a lace-trimmed fabric 'flower', with delicate feathers in a co-ordinating colour. The underside has a channel for an Alice band, but you could omit this and attach a hair slide or one or two hair combs to the fascinator instead.

You will need
1 fat quarter of printed cotton fabric
Scrap of plain cotton fabric in a contrasting colour
Round sinamay hat base, 4½in (11cm) diameter
Sewing thread to match fabric
Plastic-coated wire, 9½in (24cm) long
Four stripped coque feathers, to match contrast fabric
Self-covering button, ¾in (19mm) diameter
Lace, 9½ x ⅝in (24 x 1.5cm)
Narrow Alice band, slide or comb
Pencil, dressmaker's chalk or fabric marker
Ruler
Dressmaking scissors
General-purpose scissors
Flat-nosed pliers
Sewing needle
Iron and ironing board

Finished size is roughly:
4½in (11cm) diameter

NOTE: The round sinamay hat base is a traditional shape for fascinators. Sinamay is a natural product, woven from the processed stalks of a banana palm native to the Philippines. The fibre is three times stronger than cotton or silk.

1 Mark out and cut the following from the fat quarter of fabric: four circles 4¾in (12cm) in diameter (use a CD as a template); one circle 8½in (22cm) in diameter; one strip 9½ x 1¼in (24 x 3cm); one strip 20½ x 1¾in (52 x 4.5cm); and one strip 5 x 1½in (13 x 4cm). Cut a circle 1½in (4cm) in diameter from the scrap of contrast fabric.

2 Fold each of the four 4¾in (12cm) circles in half and in half again to form a quarter circle, then press with a hot iron. Fold the longest of the three strips in half lengthways, matching the two long edges; press. Fold the long edges of the other two strips in to meet in the centre; press.

3 The large circle is used to cover the sinamay hat base. Thread a needle with a double strand of sewing thread and sew a running stitch all round (see page 17), turning a scant ⅛in (2–3mm) of fabric to the wrong side as you do so and stitching through both layers of fabric to create a neat edge.

4 Place the hat base in the centre on the wrong side and pull up the threads to gather the edge and enclose the hat base. Secure the thread and fasten off.

5 On each of the four folded circles, with a double strand of sewing thread, sew a running stitch along the curved edge. Pull up the threads to gather, then secure the thread and fasten off. These will form the leaves for the floral decoration.

6 Using flat-nosed pliers, bend over each end of the plastic-coated wire by about ¼in (6mm).

7 Place the wire down the centre of the strip that measures 9½ x 1¼in (24 x 3cm), where the two long edges meet. Wrap the strip around the wire, with one of the folded edges on top, and slipstitch (see page 17) this folded edge and the short ends in place; when you have finished stitching, the whole of the wire will be covered with fabric. This forms the stem of the flower.

8 Attach the feathers to the fabric-covered stem. Use a single strand of thread to match the fabric and oversew (see page 17) the feather quills so that they are securely attached. You may have to trim the quills to fit.

9 Stitch the stem in place on the hat base, just off centre. Then sew the four leaves in place, two on either side of the stem.

10 To make the flower, place the lace on top of the largest strip of fabric, then sew a running stitch, using a double strand of sewing thread, parallel to the raw edge. Pull up the threads to gather the strip.

11 Arrange the gathered strip to form a spiral with two layers, one on top of the other. Secure the flower in the centre of the four leaves and stitch in place, taking the needle and thread through the centre of the flower, right through the hat base and back up again. Do this several times so that the flower is securely held in place. Use the plain fabric circle to cover the button and sew this in the centre of the flower.

12 The remaining strip of fabric forms a channel for the Alice band. Place it on the underside of the hat base and stitch the two long folded edges to the fabric inside the base. Turn under the two short ends to neaten them, but leave them unstitched so that you can slip the Alice band through the opening.

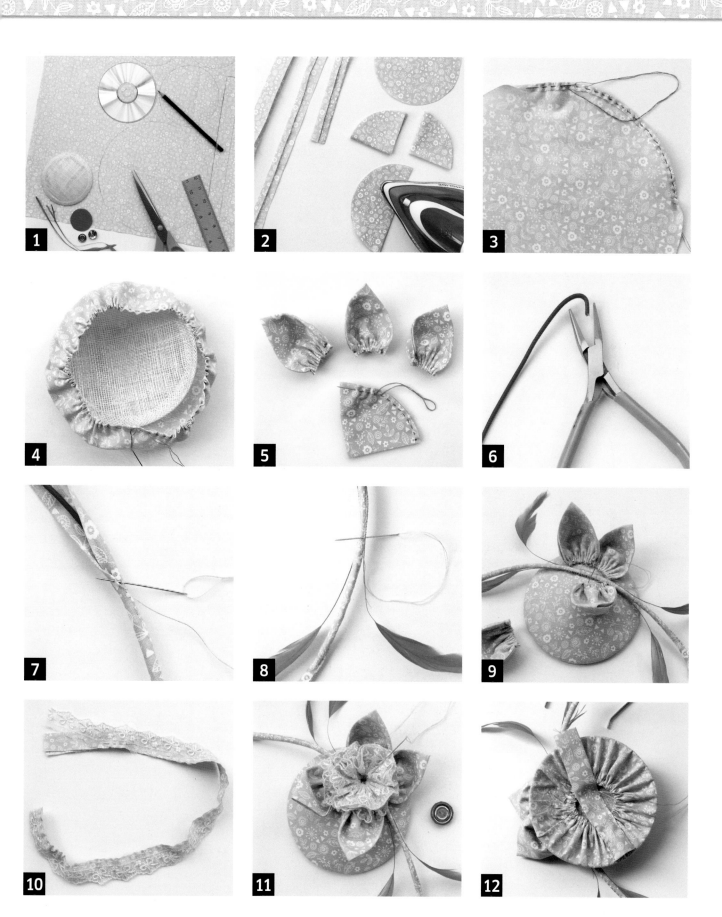

BROOCHES &
CORSAGES

MEDAL

Do you know someone who deserves a medal — perhaps for services to sewing or for simply being there for you when you need them? Made from scraps from your workbox, this is an easy project to honour someone special.

Find the template on page 138

You will need
2 fat quarters of printed cotton fabric,
    contrasting prints
Fusible bonding web,
    approximately 6 x 3in (16 x 8cm)
Felt square, approximately 2¾in (7cm)
Six-stranded embroidery thread (floss) to match fabrics
Sewing thread to match fabric
Plastic or metal closed ring, ⅝in (1.5cm) diameter
18in (45cm) length of fancy cord
Kilt pin with two rings attached
Tracing paper
Pen or pencil
Ruler
Dressmaking scissors
4in (10cm) embroidery hoop
Crewel needle
Sewing needle
Iron and ironing board

Finished size is roughly:
7in (17cm)

NOTE: The kilt pin used here has two loops for attaching charms. You could use a plain pin if you prefer, adding jump rings for attaching the top of the medal.

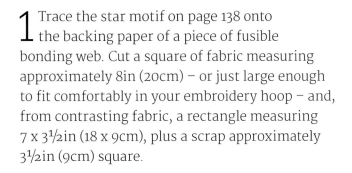

1 Trace the star motif on page 138 onto the backing paper of a piece of fusible bonding web. Cut a square of fabric measuring approximately 8in (20cm) – or just large enough to fit comfortably in your embroidery hoop – and, from contrasting fabric, a rectangle measuring 7 x 3½in (18 x 9cm), plus a scrap approximately 3½in (9cm) square.

2 Following the manufacturer's instructions, apply the bonding web to the wrong side of the 3½in (9cm) square of fabric (see page 17).

3 Cut out the star shape, peel off the backing paper and fuse it to the centre of the large square of fabric with a hot, dry iron.

4 Place the fabric in an embroidery hoop and, using two strands of embroidery thread (floss), outline the shape in blanket stitch (see page 18).

5 Draw a circle 2¼in (5.5cm) in diameter on the paper backing of a piece of fusible bonding web. Fuse this to the reverse of the appliqué, with the star shape centred in the circle. Put to one side while you make the top part of the medal.

6 Fold the strip of contrast fabric in half lengthways and stitch down its length with a ⅜in (1cm) seam allowance. Press the seam open, turn right side out and position the seam down the centre of one side. Press.

7 Fold the piece in half and push both long edges in at this point so that they meet; press.

8 Slip the ring onto the strip, pushing it down to the narrow part at the centre.

9 Cut the cord into three equal lengths. Pass one length through each of the two rings on the kilt pin and knot the ends of each one together, close to the rings. Place the ends between the two layers of fabric.

10 Slipstitch (see page 17) the edges of the fabric strip together all round. Loop the third length of cord through the ring, then pull the ends of the cord through the loop.

11 Cut out the circle and peel off the paper backing, then place it towards the top of the piece of felt, with the ends of the cord sandwiched in between. Press with a hot iron to fuse the layers together. Cut out the circle.

12 Using two strands of embroidery thread, work blanket stitch around the circle and the fabric strip.

Tip

Though it is not shown in the pictures on the opposite page, it is a good idea to lay a piece of non-stick baking parchment on top of the fusible bonding web, as this will protect the sole plate of your iron from molten glue.

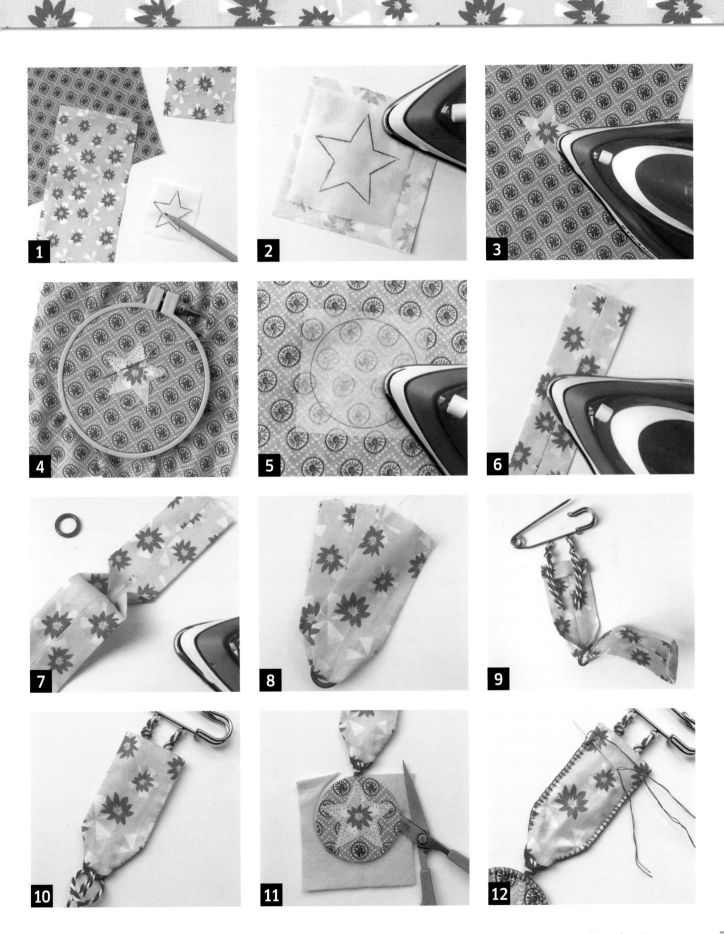

VALENTINE BROOCH

Wear your heart on your sleeve – or your lapel or collar! The brooch shown here features Valentine-themed charms (a tiny flower and heart, and a cheeky Cupid complete with bow and arrow), but you can customize yours in any way you wish.

Find the template on page 139

You will need
Scraps of printed cotton fabric, two contrasting patterns
Fusible bonding web, small piece
Six-stranded embroidery thread (floss)
    in your own choice of colours
Sewing thread to match fabric
Silver-plated jewellery wire, 0.6mm gauge, 10in (25cm) length
Six jump rings, 7mm diameter
Tube bead, 2in (5cm) in length
Kilt pin
Two small metal charms
Pencil
Tracing paper
Ruler
Dressmaking scissors
Embroidery hoop, 4in (10cm) diameter
Crewel needle
Sewing needle
Wire cutters
Round-nosed pliers
Flat-nosed pliers
Iron and ironing board

Finished size is roughly:
4in (10.5cm)

NOTE: The tube bead is functional as well as decorative, acting as a stretcher to keep the top edge of the fabric pendant from sagging. If you can't find a single bead of this length, thread two or more short tube-shaped beads, or a row of round beads, onto the wire, adding up to the required length.

VALENTINE BROOCH

1 Trace the heart shape on page 139 onto the paper backing of a piece of fusible bonding web.

2 Following the manufacturer's instructions, apply the bonding web to the wrong side of a piece of fabric, using a hot iron (see page 17). Cut out around the outline of the heart shape.

3 Peel off the backing paper and place the heart motif in the centre of a piece of contrast fabric. Fuse in place with a hot iron.

4 Place the fabric in an embroidery hoop. Thread a crewel needle with two strands of embroidery thread (floss) and work blanket stitch (see page 18) all round the edge of the heart shape.

5 With a different-coloured thread, work a border of chain stitch (see page 18) all round the shape.

6 Work a second border of chain stitch in a different colour, followed by a border of blanket stitch, with the straight 'legs' of the stitches radiating out all round.

7 Remove the fabric from the hoop and press. Cut a 3¼in (8cm) square from the fabric, with the heart motif in the centre. Cut another square the same size from the contrast fabric.

8 Fold over ½in (12mm) to the wrong side on the top and bottom edges; press. Fold the same amount under on the two side edges; press. Do the same with the contrast square.

9 Cut two 3½in (9cm) lengths of wire and curl both ends into double loops using round-nosed pliers. Lay the wires inside the side hems, one on each side, and fold the fabric over so that the loops protrude at either end. Sew a running stitch close to the fold to hold the wires in place.

10 Place the two fabric pieces wrong sides together and oversew (see page 17) the edges together with small, neat stitches.

11 Cut a 2¾in (7cm) length of wire. Coil one end into a loop, feed the wire through the long bead, and curl the emerging end into a loop.

12 Use four jump rings to attach the tube bead to the kilt pin and the fabric. To do this, hold the jump ring between your finger and thumb and use flat-nosed pliers to open it (see page 14). Feed the jump ring through one of the loops at the top of the square and the loop at the end of the bead, and close it again. Open another jump ring in the same way, feed it through the loop at the other end of the tube bead, and over the bar of the kilt pin, and close it. Repeat this process on the other side. Use the remaining two jump rings to attach the charms to the lower corners.

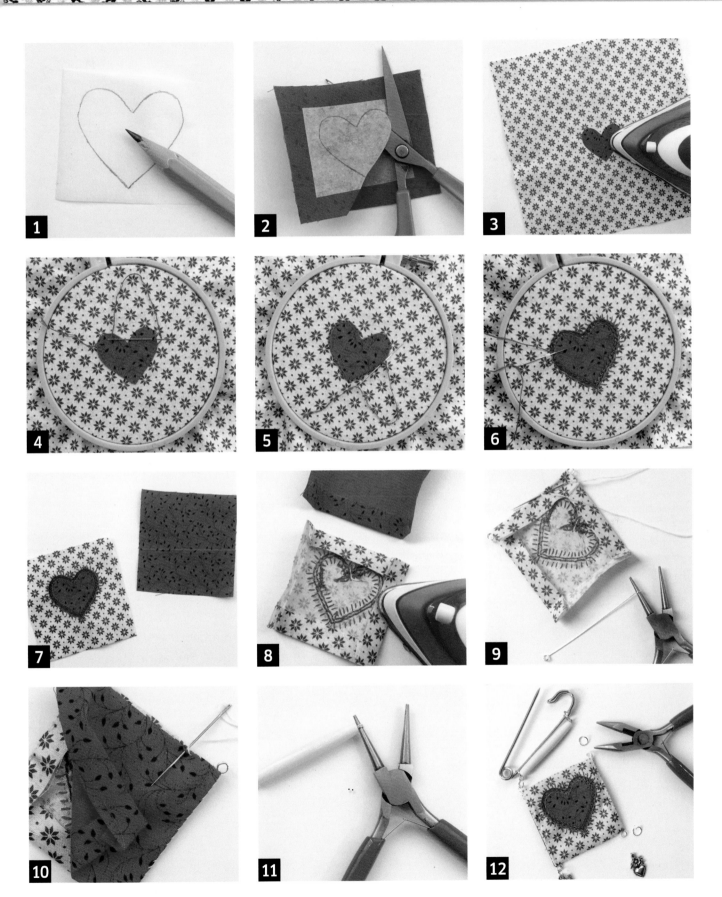

CAMEO BROOCH

A precious family portrait photo is the centrepiece for this charming brooch.
Choose a fabric with a small print for a dainty effect.

Find the template on page 140

You will need

1 fat quarter of printed cotton fabric

A4 sheet of cotton poplin photo fabric

Felt, approximately 4 x 3$\frac{1}{8}$in (10 x 8cm)

Fusible bonding web, approximately 4 x 3$\frac{1}{8}$in (10 x 8cm)

Six-stranded embroidery thread (floss) to match
   or contrast with fabric

Sewing thread to match fabric

Brooch pin

Pencil

Dressmaking scissors

Sewing needle

Crewel needle

Loop turner

Iron and ironing board

NOTE: Cotton photo fabric consists of a sheet of fabric with a paper backing attached, designed for use with a computer inkjet printer. You simply feed the fabric sheet through the printer, in the same way as regular paper. Once the paper backing has been peeled away, you can use the printed fabric in your sewing project.

Finished size is roughly:
3$\frac{1}{2}$ x 2$\frac{3}{4}$in (9 x 7cm)

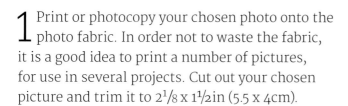
1 Print or photocopy your chosen photo onto the photo fabric. In order not to waste the fabric, it is a good idea to print a number of pictures, for use in several projects. Cut out your chosen picture and trim it to $2\frac{1}{8}$ x $1\frac{1}{2}$in (5.5 x 4cm).

2 Trace the double oval from page 140 onto the paper backing of the fusible bonding web.

3 Cut a rectangle of fabric measuring $4\frac{3}{4}$ x 4in (12 x 10cm). Following the manufacturer's instructions, apply the bonding web to the wrong side of the fabric using a hot, dry iron.

4 Cut out the shape around the outline, then cut out the centre to create a frame.

5 Peel away the paper backing from the photo fabric and place it centrally, right side up, on the felt. Peel away the paper backing from the frame and place this on top, right side up. Fuse the frame in place with a hot iron; this will also fuse the three layers together.

6 Cut out around the outer edge of the frame.

7 Thread the crewel needle with two strands of embroidery thread (floss) and embroider a blanket stitch (see page 18) around both the inner and outer edges of the frame, passing the needle through all thicknesses of fabric.

8 Cut a piece of fabric measuring 14 x 2in (36 x 5cm). Fold it in half lengthways, right sides together, and stitch down the length with a $\frac{3}{4}$in (1cm) seam allowance. Turn right side out, using a loop turner (see page 21).

9 Press the fabric strip, with the seam down the centre, and tie it into a neat bow. Trim the ends to the desired length and tuck the raw edges to the inside, closing the gap with a few slipstitches (see page 17).

10 Stitch the bow to the top of the frame, securing it in place with a few discreet stitches, using a thread to match the fabric.

11 Sew the brooch pin in place at the top of the frame, securing it to the back of the bow.

BUTTERFLY BROOCH

Nature is a great source of design ideas and, when it comes to shape, colour and pattern, butterflies are particularly inspirational. This butterfly brooch can be made in an unlimited combination of colours, patterns and fabrics, so let yourself loose with a bag of fabric scraps and see what emerges.

Find the templates on page 139

Tip

For the butterfly's antennae, choose a rigid thread that will not droop: the thread used here is a goldwork Japan thread. You could also use a length of fine wire.

Finished size is roughly:
3³/₈ x 4in (8.5 x 10cm)

You will need
Fusible bonding web, approximately 14 x 4in (35 x 10cm)
Printed cotton fabric, at least 4¹/₂ x 3¹/₂in (11 x 9cm)
Sheer fabric, at least 4 x 3¹/₄in (10 x 8cm)
2 scraps of silk fabric, each at least 3¹/₄ x 1¹/₂in (8 x 4cm)
Plain or patterned cotton fabric, at least 10in (25cm) square
Printed cotton fabric contrast fabric,
   at least 6³/₄ x 2¹/₂in (17 x 6cm)
Scrap of velvet fabric, at least 3¹/₂ x 1in (9 x 2.5cm)
Six-stranded embroidery thread (floss) to contrast
   or co-ordinate with fabrics
Sewing thread to match fabric
Matchstick
Rigid gold thread
Two small beads
Brooch pin
Tracing paper
Pencil
General-purpose scissors
Dressmaking scissors
Pinking shears
Embroidery hoop, 8in (20cm) diameter
Crewel needle
Sewing machine (optional)
Iron and ironing board
Non-stick baking parchment

1 Trace the templates from page 139 onto the paper backing of fusible bonding web. Cut out each shape roughly, leaving a small margin all round the pencil outline.

2 Place each piece, paper side up, on the wrong side of your chosen fabrics. Place the larger butterfly on the printed cotton, the smaller butterfly on sheer fabric and the two smaller shapes on two different silk fabrics. Use a hot iron without steam to bond the pieces to the fabrics, sandwiching the fabrics between two pieces of non-stick baking parchment to protect the ironing board and the sole plate of the iron.

3 Cut out the shapes along the pencil outlines you have drawn.

4 Peel off the paper backing from the two smaller shapes. Place the larger printed cotton butterfly in the centre of the 10in (25cm) square of fabric, with the smaller sheer fabric butterfly on top. Fuse in place using a hot iron. Place one silk shape across the top pair of wings and the other across the lower pair of wings. Fuse in place.

5 Place the fabric in the embroidery hoop, with the butterfly centred within the hoop. If you are going to add embroidery stitches by hand, place the fabric on top of the plain hoop and place the hoop with the screw on top. If you are going to add machine stitching, place the fabric in the hoop so that the fabric lies flat on the work surface.

6 Add decorative lines of stitching, by hand or machine, all over the butterfly's wings. Use one or two strands of thread (floss) if you're embroidering by hand. Remove the fabric from the hoop and cut out the shape using pinking shears to create a zigzag border of backing fabric all round the butterfly.

7 For the butterfly's body, you will need a strip of printed fabric measuring 6 x 1½in (15 x 4cm). Instead of cutting this, tear it so that the edges are frayed. Cut a strip of velvet measuring 3½ x 1in (9 x 2.5cm). Using general-purpose scissors, cut the head off the matchstick.

8 Place the matchstick at one end of the printed cotton strip and roll the fabric tightly around it. Before you get to the end of the strip, place the velvet strip right side down on the wrong side of the fabric and continue rolling, turning in the edges of the velvet about halfway through to create a tapered shape.

9 When you have finished rolling, pin the end of the velvet in place. Cut a 20in (50cm) length of embroidery thread. Separate three strands, thread these into a crewel needle, and stitch the end of the velvet strip in place. Do not cut the thread.

10 Wrap the thread round and round the butterfly's body, then fasten off by taking the needle right through the fabric several times to secure the end of the thread. Thread the remaining three strands of thread into the needle and repeat the process.

11 Cut a 4in (10cm) length of rigid gold thread and knot the ends. Fold the thread in half to form a V-shape for the antennae and stitch the fold to one end of the body. This is the head end of the butterfly and the stitching will be hidden when the body is attached to the wings. Sew a bead to the end of each antenna.

12 Place the body in the centre of the wings and stitch it securely in place. On the back of the brooch, stitch a brooch pin in the centre, towards the head end.

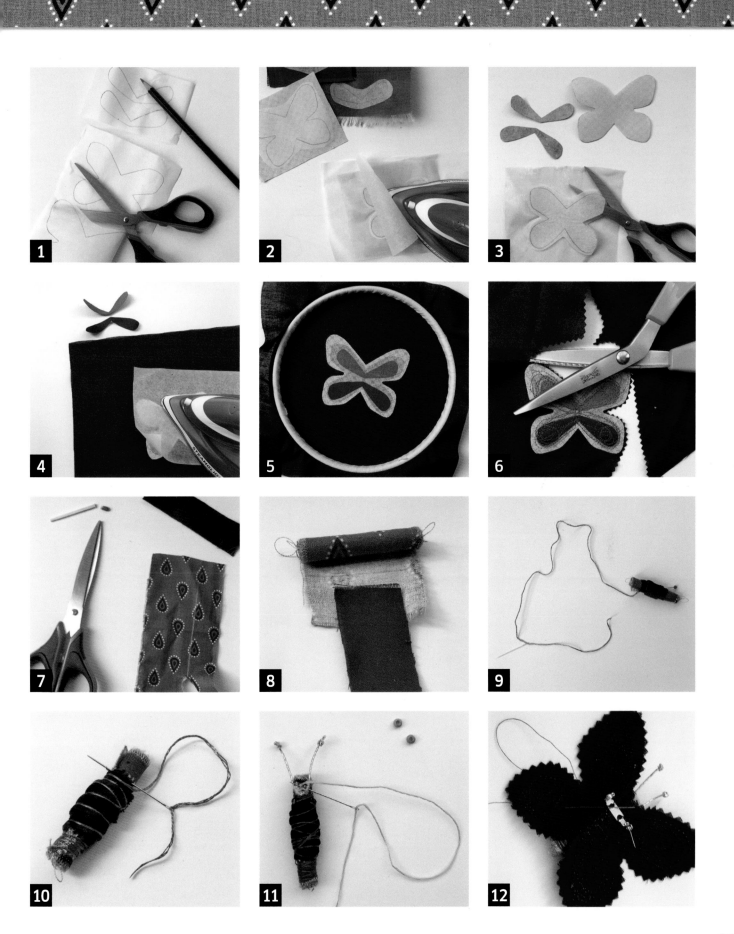

FLOWER CORSAGE

Corsages aren't just for weddings and high-school proms: you can add colour and style to almost any outfit with a fabric flower made in your own unique combination of colours and fabrics.

Find the template on page 140

You will need
Fat quarters of printed cotton fabric, six different prints
Scrap of felt
Six small beads
Six-stranded embroidery thread (floss) in your own choice of colours
Button or other round object, 1¼in (3cm) diameter
Safety pin
Sewing thread to match the fabric
Pen or pencil
Ruler
Dressmaking scissors
Corner and edge shaper
Crewel needle
Sewing needle or sewing machine
Iron and ironing board
Fabric glue (optional)

NOTE: Instead of the safety pin used here, you could use a brooch pin like the one shown on the Butterfly Brooch on page 80.

Finished size is roughly:
6¼ x 5³/8in (16 x 13.5cm)

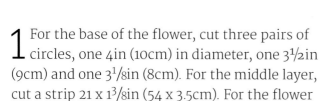

1 For the base of the flower, cut three pairs of circles, one 4in (10cm) in diameter, one 3½in (9cm) and one 3⅛in (8cm). For the middle layer, cut a strip 21 x 1⅜in (54 x 3.5cm). For the flower centre, cut a strip 13 x 1½in (33 x 4cm).

2 With right sides together, stitch pairs of circles together with a ¼in (6mm) seam allowance, leaving a gap of approximately 1in (2.5cm) for turning. Turn right side out, using a corner and edge shaper to push out the circles neatly (see page 21). Tuck in the raw edges on the openings, and press.

3 Thread a crewel needle with two strands of embroidery thread (floss) in a contrasting colour and sew a decorative running stitch (see page 17) around each circle, close to the edge.

4 Stack the three circles on top of one another in order of size. Using a button or similar round object as a template, draw a circle 1¼in (3cm) in diameter on the top of the stack.

5 Stitching through all layers, work running stitch around the outline you have drawn.

6 Fold the long strip of fabric in half lengthways and, with double sewing thread, stitch a gathering stitch (see page 17) along its length, close to the raw edges.

7 Pull up the threads to gather the strip and stitch the gathered edge around the outside of the circle that you stitched in step 5. Coil it round into a loose spiral as you stitch, then fasten off the thread securely.

8 Fold in the two long edges of the shorter strip to meet at the centre, then fold the strip in half lengthways with the raw edges inside. Attach one end of the strip to the centre of the corsage with a few stitches. Twisting the strip as you go and coiling it into a spiral, stitch it in place to form the centre of the flower.

9 Stitch a cluster of beads in the centre of the flower.

10 Cut a strip of fabric 8 x 1¼in (20 x 3cm) for a stem, fold it in half lengthways and stitch down its length with a ¼in (6mm) seam allowance. Turn right side out and tuck in the ends. Cut eight leaf shapes using the template on page 140. Stitch these together in pairs, with right sides together, ¼in (6mm) from the edges, leaving the straight edge at the base of each leaf unstitched. Turn right side out. Press all pieces.

11 Fold the stem in half and stitch it to the back of the flower. Embroider veins on each leaf using running stitch and two strands of embroidery thread, then stitch the base of each leaf in place.

12 Stitch the safety pin, slightly off centre, to a 1½in (4cm) circle of felt. Sew or stick the felt to the back of the flower, in the centre.

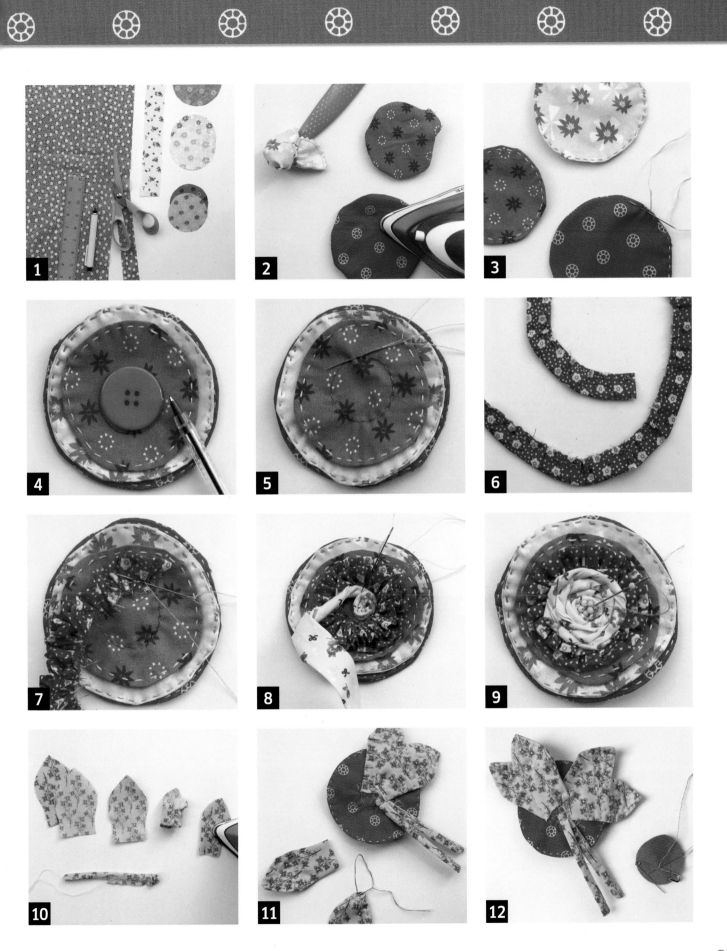

JEWELLERY

TASSEL EARRINGS

Bold statement earrings can be a bit heavy to wear – but because these are made from fabric, they are light as a feather. Little silver ball charms dangle just below the tassel, like the stamens of an exotic flower.

You will need
1 fat quarter of cotton fabric
2 wooden beads, ¾in (2cm) diameter, with large holes
4 bead end caps for the wooden beads
2 conical metal bead caps, approximately ¾in (2cm) long
    with a ⅝in (1.5cm) diameter
Silver wire, 0.6mm gauge, approximately 20in (50cm) length
8 jump rings, 4mm diameter
2 metal spacer beads
2 medium round beads
6 small round beads
8 small metal ball charms
Pair of ear wires
Sewing thread to match fabric
Dressmaking scissors
Bodkin or blunt tapestry needle
Fabric glue
Sewing needle
Wire cutters
Round-nosed pliers
Flat-nosed pliers
Iron and ironing board

Finished size is roughly:
5¹/8 x 1¹/8in (13 x 3cm)

NOTE: The style of earring fitting shown here is sometimes called a fish hook or French hook. You could use another type if you prefer, and for non-pierced eras you would need a clip fitting: various types are available.

1 For the ball part of the earrings, cut two strips of fabric measuring 20 x $^3/_8$in (50 x 1cm). Press well. You will also need the two wooden beads and a bodkin or blunt needle with a large eye.

Tip

This works best with a fabric that is similar on both sides, as the wrong side will be visible.

2 Thread one end of a fabric strip into the eye of the needle and tie a single knot to keep it in place.

3 Start wrapping the fabric around the bead by inserting the needle through the hole. Each wrap should overlap the preceding one. There is no need to glue the end of the fabric to the bead, as the wrapping process will hold it in place.

4 When the bead is completely covered, cut off the excess fabric.

5 Secure the fabric end to the inside of the bead with a small dot of fabric glue. Repeat steps 2–5 for the second earring.

6 For the tassel part of the earring, cut two pieces of fabric measuring 10 x 1$^3/_8$in (25 x 3.5cm). Press well. With a double length of sewing thread, sew a running stitch close to one long edge of each fabric strip.

7 Pull up the thread and coil the gathered strip into a tight spiral. Secure it with a few stitches at the top. Cut the thread and push the gathered end up into the conical bead cap. Secure it in place with a dab of glue. Repeat for the second tassel.

8 Cut six lengths of wire, each approximately 2$^3/_4$in (7cm) long. With round-nosed pliers, curl one end of each wire to create a closed ring. Put two wires aside for later. Join two pairs of wires using a jump ring (see page 14) and push one end of the wire up inside the tassel.

9 Thread beads onto the top wire: one small round bead, one slightly larger round bead, and a metal spacer bead. Trim the wire, if necessary, so that about $^5/_8$in (1.5cm) protrudes above the beads when you pull the wire up tightly. Coil the wire to create a closed ring.

10 Trim the bottom wire, if necessary, so that about $^5/_8$in (1.5cm) protrudes below the fabric tassel. Coil the wire to create a closed ring. Open a jump ring, attach four small charms, loop the jump ring through the closed ring at the bottom of the tassel, then close the jump ring.

11 Thread beads onto the reserved wires in this order: a small round bead, a spacer bead, a bead end cap with the cup facing upwards, the fabric-covered bead, another bead cap with the cup facing downwards and another small bead. Coil the straight end of the wire into a closed ring. Attach a jump ring to each end of the wire and link one end to the top of the tassel and the other to the ear wire, as shown.

BUTTON EARRINGS

If you're a hoarder who likes to use up every small scrap of fabric and has jars of old buttons just waiting to be repurposed with panache, then these chunky earrings will be right up your street!

You will need
Scraps of various printed cotton fabrics
9 pairs of sew-through buttons, assorted sizes,
    from $^9/_{16}$ to 1in (1.4 to 2.5cm)
Thread to match fabric
Silver wire, 0.6mm gauge
4 disc beads
4 round beads
4 jump rings, 4mm diameter
Pair of ear wires
2 small flower-shaped charm beads
Circle templates or pair of compasses
Pencil
Dressmaking scissors
Sewing needle
Wire cutters
Round-nosed pliers
Flat-nosed pliers
Iron and ironing board

NOTE: The largest pieces of fabric needed for this project are no larger than 2in (5cm) square and the smallest a mere 1¼in (3cm), so this project really is perfect for using up small scraps.

Finished size is roughly:
4 x 1in (10 x 2.5cm)

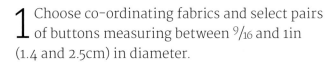
1 Choose co-ordinating fabrics and select pairs of buttons measuring between ⁹/₁₆ and 1in (1.4 and 2.5cm) in diameter.

2 Mark out pairs of circles on the fabric pieces, using a pencil. Each fabric circle should be twice the diameter of the button it will cover.

3 Cut out the circles, press, and sew a running stitch around each one. Place a button in the centre, pull up the threads to gather the fabric, and fasten off.

4 For each earring, cut a piece of wire approximately 11in (28cm) in length. Using round-nosed pliers, curl a double loop in the centre of the wire.

5 Grip the loop using flat-nosed pliers and twist the two wire ends together for about ¼in (6mm).

6 Push the two wire ends through the hole in one of the disc beads and then through one of the round beads. Push the two beads down over the twist in the wire.

7 Thread the covered buttons onto the wires, threading one wire through each of the two holes in each button. Start with the smallest button and increase in size until you get to the largest button in the centre, then decrease in size.

8 Push both wires through a round bead and then through a disc bead. Cut off the excess wire so that approximately 1¼in (3cm) protrudes from the top of the stack. Curl these two strands, using round-nosed pliers, until they meet the top disc bead, pressing the coil of wire against the bead to slightly compress the stack of buttons.

9 Attach a jump ring to each end of the wire (see page 14) and link an ear wire to one end and a small flower-shaped charm to the other.

NOTE: Jewellery wire is available in various thicknesses, or 'gauges'. A 0.6mm gauge is easy to work with and ideal for items such as these earrings. It is usually available to purchase in a roll from which you cut off the length you require, using wire cutters. The smallest roll is typically about 3 metres long.

TIP

A pair of compasses is an invaluable tool for drawing circles of various diameters. Or you may wish to invest in a plastic template, which is a useful addition to any workbox.

SHOE BOWS

Perfect for pimping the plainest pair of pumps, when it comes to accessorizing your outfits, shoe bows are a great item to have at your disposal. So quick and easy to make, you could create lots of sets, so you're ready for a quick change at a moment's notice.

You will need
1 fat quarter of printed cotton fabric
1 fat quarter of plain cotton fabric
2 shoe clips
Faux jewels
Thread to match fabric
Dressmaker's chalk pencil
Ruler
Dressmaking scissors
General-purpose scissors
Sewing needle
Sewing machine (optional)
Loop turner
All-purpose glue
Iron and ironing board

NOTE: Faux jewels are available in a range of sizes, shapes and colours. The flat back allows them to be stuck onto various materials, including fabric. For this, choose a glue that is recommended for sticking metal components to fabric. Some of these jewels have a hot-melt glue on the flat back and can be stuck in place using a specially designed electric heated wand.

Finished size is roughly:
3in (8cm) from end to end of bow

1 Place the two fabrics together. Measure and mark out two strips, each 21 x 1½in (53 x 4cm), and cut these out from both fabrics. You will have two plain strips and two patterned strips, one pair for each shoe bow.

2 With right sides together, and with a ⁵⁄₁₆in (8mm) seam allowance, stitch down one long side, across one end at an angle, and down the other long side, leaving the other short end open. Cut off the excess fabric at the stitched end.

3 Trim the seam allowance to reduce bulk. Using a loop turner (see page 21), turn each tube of fabric right side out. With the seamline down the centre of one side, press with a hot iron.

4 From this long strip, starting at the open end, measure and cut one 7in (18cm) length and one 6¼in (16cm) length. These two pieces will form the bow loops. On the remaining piece, measure 4¾in (12cm) from the pointed end and draw a diagonal mark across the width of the fabric.

5 Cut along the mark you have drawn. The larger of the two angled pieces will form the bow tail and the smaller piece will wrap around the centre of the bow.

6 For one bow, take one 7in (18cm) length and one 6¼in (16cm) length. Gather each end of the strips with a running stitch (see page 17), using the thread doubled for extra strength, so that it doesn't break when you pull up the stitches to gather the fabric, then wrap thread around the centre.

7 To form the bow loops, bring the gathered ends to the centre on each piece and secure with a few stitches, taking your needle through all layers of fabric.

8 For each bow, place the smaller looped piece on top of the larger one. Stitch together, then wrap the sewing thread round and round the centre and pull tightly before fastening off.

9 To make the tails for each bow, first tuck in the fabric at the cut end and slipstitch (see page 17) the folded edges together, to neaten the end. Then fold the two ends across the strip and pin in place.

10 Place one of the prepared bow loop pairs on top of one of the tail pieces. Stitch in place through the centre of the bow. Then cut off the angled end of the remaining short pieces and wrap one around the centre of each bow to cover the join. Overlap the ends and sew in place; this join will be at the back of the bow and will be covered by the metal shoe clip.

11 Stitch a shoe clip to the back of each bow. Open up the clip before stitching: the hinged part, with the teeth that grip onto the shoe, should be at the top of the bow. When sewing, take the needle through the holes in the clip and through the fabric. Make sure the clips are securely attached.

12 As a finishing touch, stick a small cluster of faux jewels to the centre of each bow. Here, a central light blue jewel is surrounded by six brighter blue jewels, resembling sapphires, to form a flower shape.

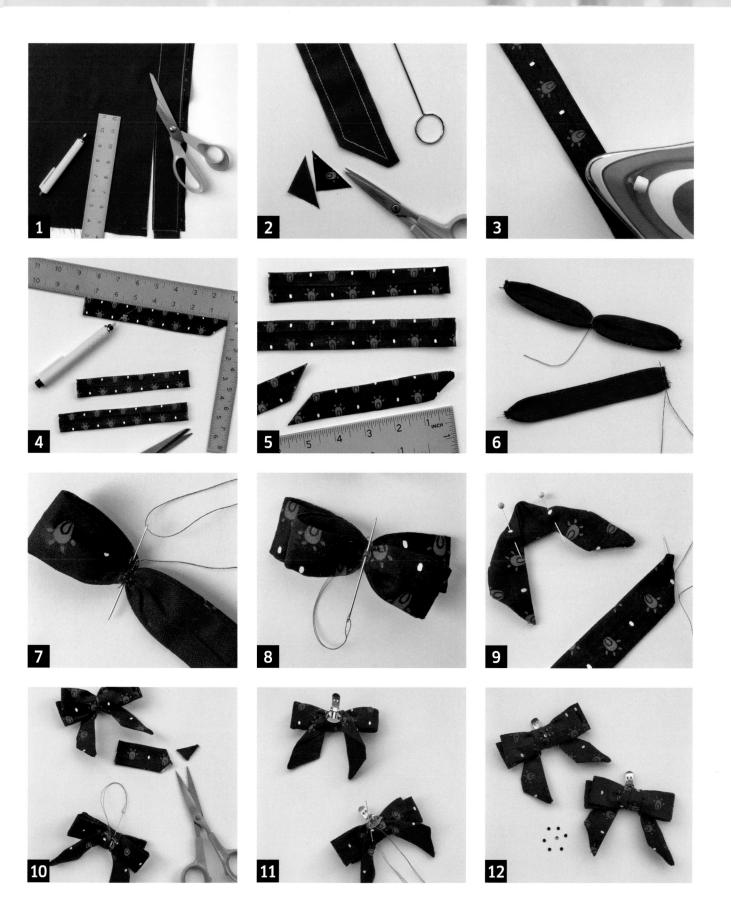

WRAPPED BANGLE

Give a chunky bangle that's seen better days a new lease of life by wrapping it in colourful fabric. Charity shops, markets and car boot sales are treasure troves of unloved and unwanted jewellery and this simple design makes a great and inexpensive gift – if you can bear to part with it!

You will need
1 fat quarter of printed cotton fabric
Chunky bangle
Thread to match fabric
Ruler
Pencil
Dressmaking scissors
Sewing needle
Iron and ironing board

NOTE: All kinds of bangles can be covered: look out for thick bangles made from plastic, wood, metal, bamboo and other materials.

1 Mark out and cut three strips along the length of the fabric, each 1¼in (3cm) wide and 20½–22in (52–56cm) long, depending on the length of your fat quarter.

2 Join the short ends of the three strips with a ³⁄₈in (1cm) seam allowance, to make one long continuous strip. Press the seams open.

3 Fold ¼in (6mm) to the wrong side along one long edge. Press.

4 Wrap one end of the fabric strip around the bangle, angling it slightly towards the right. Using a needle and thread to match the fabric, secure with a few stitches at the point where the fabric overlaps.

5 Wrap the fabric strip around the bangle, always at a slight angle, so that the raw edge of the fabric is covered by the folded edge with each wrap.

6 When you reach the starting point and the bangle is completely covered, turn under the raw edge on the remaining portion of the strip by ¼in (6mm) and press.

7 Wrap this folded, tapered end around so that the end is on the inside of the bangle. (You may wish to trim off any excess before you do so.) Neatly stitch the folded end to the fabric on the inside of the bangle.

Tip
If the surface of your bangle is very slippery, when you start to wrap it with fabric, you may wish to use glue or sticky tape to hold the end of the strip in place before proceeding.

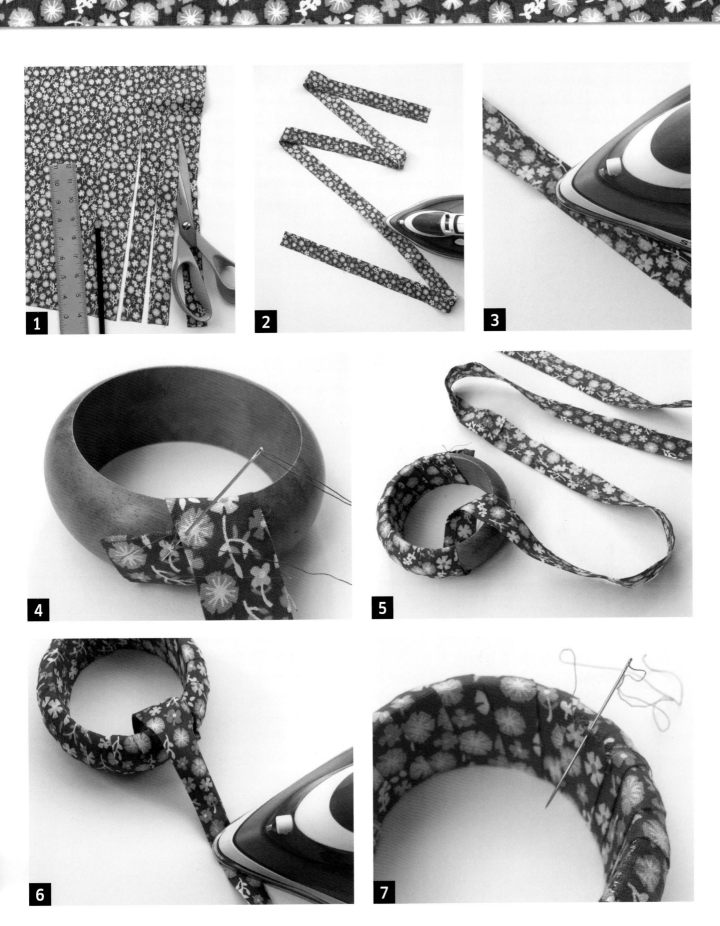

WRIST CUFF

Here's another opportunity to raid your scrap bag and button box:
this versatile accessory is great for adding a touch of colour and texture
to an outfit, or even for discreetly covering a scar or tattoo.

You will need
Scraps of printed cotton fabric,
    four or five different patterns
Selection of buttons, ¼–¾in (5–20mm) diameter
Glass seed beads
Ricrac braid, approximately 20in (50cm) length
Six-stranded embroidery thread (floss)
    in your own choice of colours
Sewing thread to match fabric
2 press fasteners
Ruler
Rotary cutter and self-healing mat (optional)
Dressmaking scissors
Sewing needle
Sewing machine (optional)
Fine sewing needle or beading needle
Iron and ironing board

NOTE: Press fasteners have been chosen as a
fastening because they make it easy to fasten
the cuff on your wrist using one hand.

Finished size is roughly:
8 x 2in (20 x 5cm),
to fit an average wrist

1 Cut a 2¾in (7cm) square of each of four different fabrics. The most accurate way to do this is using a ruler, a rotary cutter and a self-healing mat. Also cut one strip measuring 8½ x 2¾in (22 x 7cm).

2 Using a ⅜in (1cm) seam allowance, join the four squares together to make a patchwork strip. Press the seams open. Fold the two long edges to the wrong side, to meet in the centre, and press; do the same with the long strip.

3 Cut the ricrac braid into two equal lengths and stitch one piece down each long side of the strip, on the wrong side, positioning the braid so that it creates a wavy border on the right side.

4 Cut three circles 1in (2.5cm) in diameter and pin one across the centre of each seamline.

5 Stitch each circle in place, using a single strand of embroidery thread (floss). Use the tip of your needle to turn under the raw edge and slipstitch (see page 17) the folded edge to the background fabric.

6 Using a single strand of embroidery thread, stitch buttons in place. Be creative: instead of sewing them on in the conventional way, bring the needle up through the holes in the button, and down into the fabric outside the rim. And try stacking buttons on top of one another, or adding one or two small beads to the centre of a button.

7 Fold ⅜in (1cm) to the wrong side all round on each fabric piece, then place them wrong sides together. Slipstitch the folded edges together.

8 Stitch the press fasteners in place at each end of the cuff – the pointed halves on the backing strip and the recessed halves on the cuff front.

Tip

Customise the cuff by using your own selection of buttons, or by adding sequins for a bit of sparkle. You could also use a lace edging instead of ricrac braid.

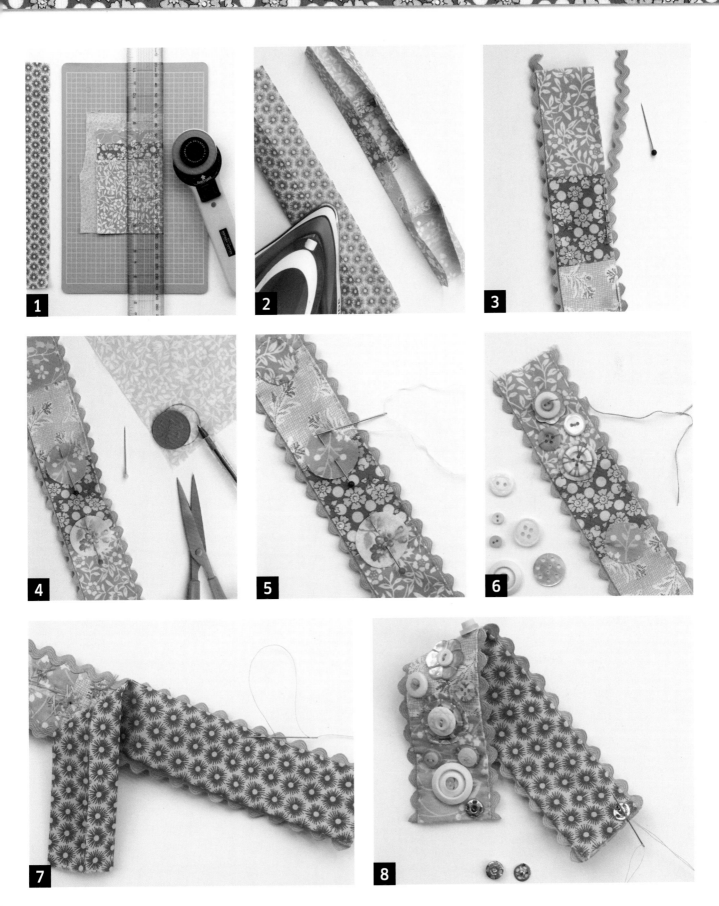

IN THE BAG

EARBUD PURSE

If you like to listen to music while you're on the move, this little purse will keep your earbuds safe and prevent the wires from getting tangled up in your bag or pocket. Alternatively, it's a handy size and shape for a small round mirror or compact, or for small change.

You will need
1 fat quarter of printed cotton fabric
1 fat quarter of contrast fabric, for lining
Fusible fleece, approximately 10in (25cm) square
Nylon zip, at least 6in (15cm) long
16in (40cm) length of bias binding, $\frac{5}{8}$in (1.5cm) wide
8mm jump ring
Silver star charm
Sewing thread to match fabric
Pencil
Dressmaking scissors
Non-stick baking parchment
Ruler
Air-erasable fabric marker pen
Pins
Sewing needle or sewing machine
Flat-nosed pliers
Iron and ironing board

NOTE: A CD, which measures $4\frac{3}{4}$in (12cm) in diameter, makes an ideal template for cutting circles.

Finished size is roughly:
5in (12.5cm) diameter

1 From each fat quarter, mark out and cut two circles 4¾in (12cm) in diameter. From the fusible fleece, cut four circles the same size as the fabric.

2 Following the manufacturer's instructions, apply one circle of fusible fleece to the wrong side of each of the fabric circles, using a hot iron (see page 17). Place a piece of non-stick baking parchment between the iron and the fleece to protect the sole plate of the iron.

3 Using an air-erasable pen and a ruler, mark a grid of lines approximately ¾in (2cm) apart, following the grain of the fabric. Stitch along the lines you have drawn.

4 Cut two of the circles – one of each fabric – in half, making sure the cut follows the straight grain of the fabric.

5 Place one of the lining semicircles right side up, with the zip right side up on top and one of the main fabric semicircles right side down on top of the zip. Pin together. The curved edges of the semicircles should be aligned and the straight edges about ⅛in (3mm) in from the edge of the zip. Stitch along the straight edge through all layers, ¼in (6mm) from the fabric edges.

6 Repeat the process on the other side of the zip with the other two semicircles. Fold the fabric pieces away from the zip and press.

7 Topstitch (see page 20) close to the folds on either side of the zip. Slide the zip tab to the centre. Close the gap between the tapes on the open end with a few stitches.

8 Tack (see page 17) the main fabric and lining together all round, close to the raw edge, then cut off the ends of the zip level with the edges of the fabric.

9 Place the printed circle wrong side up and the lining right side up on top of it, then place the zipped section right side up on top of both, matching the raw edges all round. Pin the layers together and stitch through all layers approximately ¼in (6mm) from the edge; this stitching will be covered by the bias binding in the next step.

10 Cover the edge of the purse with bias binding (see page 21).

11 Use the jump ring to attach the silver charm to the zip pull (see page 14).

NOTE: A novelty bias binding with a decorative lacy picot edge has been used here, but you could use plain bias binding for a less fancy effect.

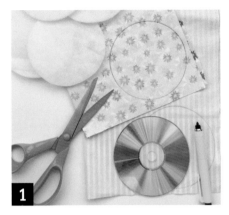

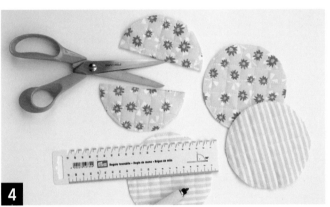

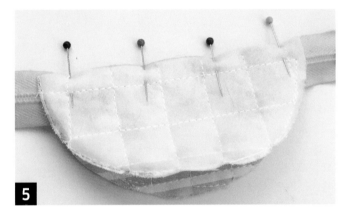

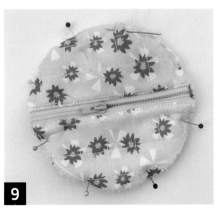

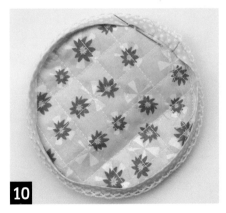

1

2

3

4

5

6

7

8

9

10

11

BAG TASSEL

An eye-catching fabric tassel in jewel-bright hues not only adds colour and texture to your bag or suitcase, it also makes it easier to identify your luggage — very useful on an airport baggage carousel, when most of the bags look the same.

You will need
Scraps of various printed cotton fabrics
Sewing thread to match fabric
Six-stranded embroidery thread (floss) in three
    different colours
Pencil
Ruler
Dressmaking scissors
Binding clips
Sewing needle
Sewing machine (optional)
Corner and edge turner or Hera marker
Safety pin
Iron and ironing board

NOTE: Use any fabric scraps for this. You can choose whether or not to theme or match the colours, or to make them completely random. When laying out the fabric pieces in step 2, you may wish to position your favourite colours and patterns on the right-hand side as these will be on the outside of the tassel.

Finished size is roughly:
5in (13cm) long, excluding loop

1 Cut six rectangles of fabric measuring 9½ x 4¾in (24 x 12cm) and one measuring 14½ x 2½in (37 x 6cm).

2 Place the long strip right side up. Fold each of the other pieces in half widthways and press. Place the first piece ¾in (2cm) in from one short end, with the fold lined up with the top of the strip. Place the remaining pieces along the strip, overlapping, about 1½in (4cm) apart.

3 Adjust the pieces, if necessary, so that they are evenly spaced and there is ¾in (2cm) of the strip exposed at either end. Hold the fabric pieces in place using binding clips.

4 Stitch across the top with a ⅝in (1.5cm) seam allowance. Press the seam up towards the strip.

5 Fold the long edge of the strip to meet the folded edges of the fabric pieces. Press. Fold again, so that the folded edge of the strip meets the seamline.

6 Slipstitch (see page 17) the folded edge to the seamline.

7 Score lines at ⅜in (1cm) intervals, from the bottom edge to the base of the top strip. Do this by scoring along a straight edge using a tool such as a corner and edge shaper or a Hera marker.

8 Cut along the score lines, through all layers, to just below the top strip, taking care not to snip through the stitches.

9 To make a loop for hanging, cut 12 lengths of embroidery thread (four each of three different colours), each 18in (45cm) long. Fold each bunch in half and make a three-stranded plait. (If you pass the bundle of strands over the bar of a safety pin, you can attach the pin to a stable object such as an ironing board, to make it easier to plait.)

10 Knot the ends of the plait together and place it at one end, with the knot just below the top strip.

11 Start to roll up the strip. Roll it tightly and stitch the edges together as you go, using small, discreet stitches from the loop end.

12 When you have rolled up the whole strip, fold in the raw end and slipstitch the fold in place neatly.

LANYARD

If your job requires you to display an ID card or a backstage pass, or you need a handy way to carry your keys, camera, USB flash drive or pen, then this lanyard will come in handy. Make it in your own combination of cotton prints and no one else will have one like it.

You will need
Three fat quarters of printed cotton fabric,
    all different
Fusible interfacing, 41 x 1¼in (104 x 3cm)
Sewing thread to match fabric
Six-stranded embroidery thread (floss) to match
    or tone with fabric
Metal lanyard end, 1¼in (3cm) wide
Chalk pencil or fabric marker
Quilter's square or ruler
Dressmaking scissors
General-purpose scissors
Flat-nosed pliers
Sewing machine
Crewel needle
Iron and ironing board

NOTE: Lanyard ends are available to buy from stockists that sell a wide range of jewellery findings. They are relatively easy to source online by searching under the heading 'key fob hardware'. The clips have teeth to grip the end of a length of braid or fabric and are available in 1in (2.5cm) and 1¼in (3cm) widths.

Finished size is roughly:
40 x 1¼in (102 x 3cm)

1 From each fat quarter, cut a strip measuring 14½ x 3¼in (36.5 x 8cm). You will now have three strips, each a different design.

2 Join the three strips together with a seam allowance of ³⁄₈in (1cm), to make one long strip. Press the seams open.

3 Place the strip of fusible interfacing down the centre of the fabric strip, on the wrong side. Press to fuse in place (see page 17).

4 Fold one side of the fabric across the interfacing and press. On the other long edge, turn under ⁵⁄₁₆in (8mm) and press, then fold this side of the fabric across the interfacing and press.

5 Thread a crewel needle with two strands of embroidery thread (floss) and sew a running stitch (see page 17) up the centre of the strip, close to the fold, to hold the fabric in place. Stitch four more lines of running stitch, evenly spaced, two on either side of the first line of stitching, using different-coloured threads.

6 Trim any loose threads from the two ends of the strip, place the ends together, one on top of the other, and insert into the lanyard clip. To close the clip, squeeze it shut using flat-nosed pliers, so that the prongs inside pierce the fabric and hold it firmly in place.

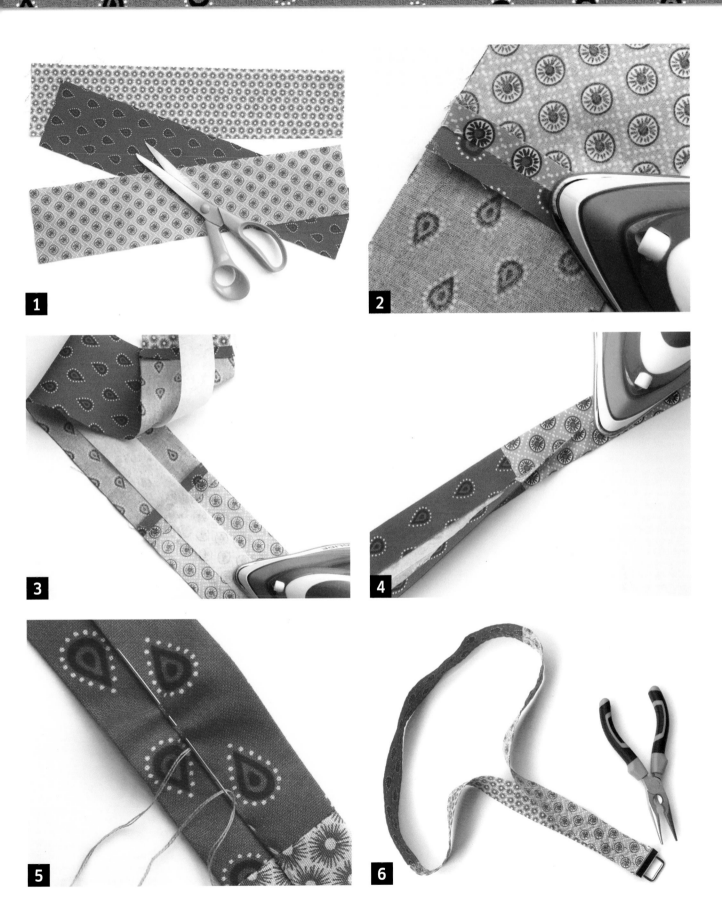

KEY FOB

Home, Sweet Home! An appliqué tag is a great way to identify your house keys and would make a lovely housewarming gift. This one is made from fabric scraps and backed with leather to make it sturdy.

Find the template on page 140

Find the template on page 140

You will need
Scraps of printed cotton fabric, five different,
   each approximately 4 x 3½in (10 x 9cm)
Plain cotton fabric, at least 8in (20cm) square
Fusible bonding web, approximately 6 x 4¾in (15 x 12cm)
Leather scrap, approximately 3 x 2½in (8 x 6cm)
4in (10cm) length of multi-coloured daisy braid
Small sequin
2¾in (7cm) length of ribbon or braid, ⅝in (1.5cm) wide
Lobster swivel clip with D-ring
Six-stranded embroidery thread (floss) in colours
   to match fabrics
Sewing thread to match fabric
Tracing paper
Pencil
Fabric glue and spreader
Dressmaking scissors
Embroidery hoop, 5in (12.5cm) diameter
Crewel needle
Fabric glue and spreader
Iron and ironing board

Finished size is roughly:
3 x 2in (7.5 x 5cm),
excluding chimney

NOTE: The lobster swivel clip shown here has a D-shaped ring to attach to the 'chimney'. The width of the bar matches the width of the braid.

1 Trace or photocopy the house motif on page 140 onto plain paper. Using a pencil, trace the individual shapes on to the paper backing of the bonding web: the whole house shape, the roof, the door, the windows and the shrubbery.

2 Roughly cut out each shape, leaving a small margin around each one. Place the shapes glue side down on the wrong side of the fabric scraps, and fuse in place with a hot, dry iron (see page 17).

3 Cut out each shape along the pencil outline, peel the backing paper from each one, and place them in position in the centre of the plain fabric. Fuse in place with a hot, dry iron.

4 Place the fabric in an embroidery hoop, with the motif in the centre. Using two strands of embroidery thread (floss), outline each shape in blanket stitch (see page 18).

5 Sew lines of backstitch (see page 19) across each window and stitch a sequin in place for a door knob. Snip several individual flowers from the daisy braid and stitch these in place.

6 Remove the fabric from the hoop and press it lightly on the reverse. Slip the ribbon through the ring on the lobster clip and place it centrally across the roof. Stitch in place, just above the top of the roofline.

7 Cut out the house shape, leaving a margin of ³⁄₈in (1cm) all round.

8 Fold the fabric border to the wrong side and press.

9 Spread a thin layer of fabric glue on the border and around the edge of the motif. Leave for 10 minutes (or according to the instructions for the glue you are using), then press the border in place with your fingertips.

10 Spread a thin layer of glue over the whole of the wrong side of the motif and all over the wrong side of the leather. Leave for 10 minutes.

11 Place the two together and press. Leave under a book or similar weight until the glue has dried, then trim away the excess leather all around the edge, taking care not to snip through the stitches.

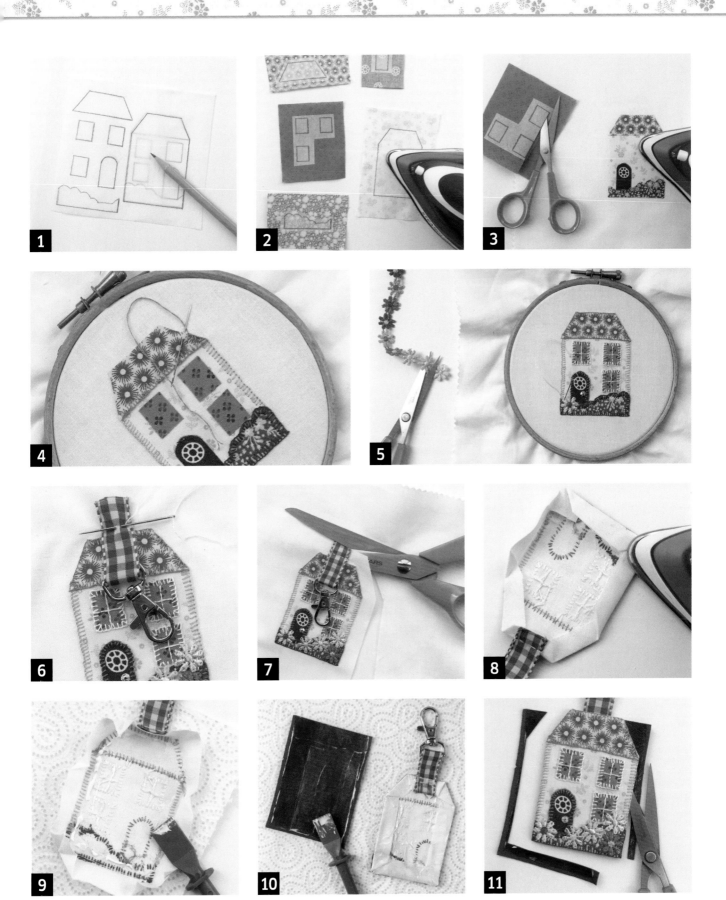

LUGGAGE LABEL

Add a touch of class to your luggage with this hand-embroidered label personalized with your initials. Choose a subtle colour palette, such as this blue stitching on a neutral grey-and-white cotton print, for style and sophistication.

Find the templates on pages 140-41

You will need
2 fat quarters of printed cotton fabric
Piece of felt, at least 6 x 4in (15 x 10cm)
20in (50cm) length of cotton bias binding, $^5/8$in (1.5cm) wide
Six-stranded embroidery thread (floss) in coral pink and pale green, or your own choice of colours
Thread to match fabric and binding
4in (10cm) ball chain, with connector
Lobster swivel clip with ring
Eyelet, $^5/8$in (1.5cm) diameter, and eyelet setting tool
4in (10cm) ball chain, with connector
Tracing paper
Water-erasable fabric marker pen
Permanent fabric marker pen or pencil
Dressmaking scissors
5in (12.5cm) embroidery hoop
Crewel needle
Pins
Sewing needle
Sewing machine (optional)
Iron and ironing board

Finished size is roughly:
5$^3/8$ x 3$^1/8$in (13.5 x 8cm)

NOTE: You will not need a whole fat quarter. A remnant measuring about 8 x 5$^1/2$in (20 x 14cm) – large enough to fit into a 5in (12.5cm) embroidery hoop – will suffice.

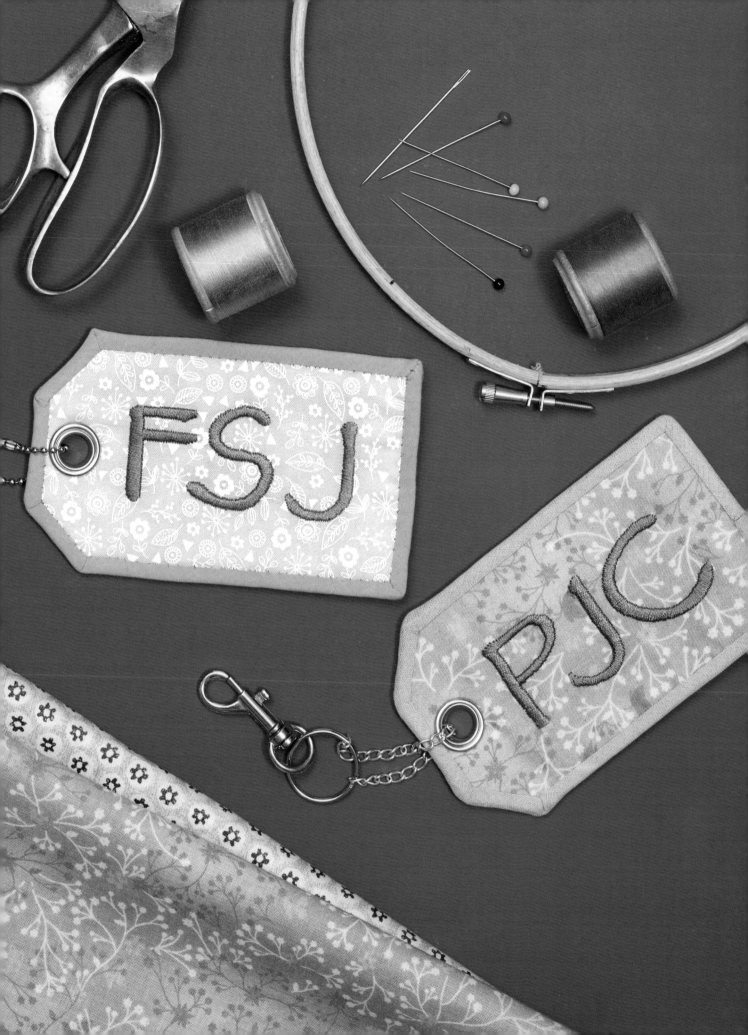

1 Cut a piece of fabric measuring approximately 8 x 5½in (20 x 14cm). Trace or photocopy the label template and your chosen initials on pages 140–41 onto plain paper, then trace them onto the centre of the fabric, using a water-soluble marker for the lettering and a permanent pen or pencil for the outline. Place the fabric in an embroidery hoop.

2 Thread a crewel needle with two strands of embroidery thread (floss). Sew two lines of running stitches (see page 17) within the outline of the letters, then fill in the letter shapes using satin stitch (see page 18).

3 Remove the fabric from the hoop, wash out the design lines using cold water and leave to dry, then press. Place the backing fabric wrong side up, with the felt on top and the embroidered fabric right side up on top of both. Pin the layers together.

4 Cut out the layers of fabric along the lines of the label.

5 Tack the layers together, close to the cut edges.

6 On the right side, line up one edge of the bias binding with the raw edge of the label and stitch along the fold by hand or machine (see page 20). When you reach a corner, make a small pleat in the binding, to help create a neat mitre (see page 21).

7 Turn the label over, fold the binding over to cover the raw edges of fabric, and slipstitch (see page 17) the folded edge of the binding in place along the seamline.

8 Mark the position of the eyelet with a cross. Cut or punch a hole in the marked position.

9 Use the setting tool to set the eyelet in place.

10 Thread the ball chain through the eyelet and the lobster swivel clip, then close the chain.

NOTE: There is a range of options for attaching the label to your luggage. Instead of a ball chain, you could use a length of linked chain with the ends slipped through a split ring. You can, if you prefer, clip the lobster swivel clip directly onto the eyelet, without using a chain. Or you could dispense with the hardware and loop a length of ribbon through the eyelet, using this to tie the label to your bag.

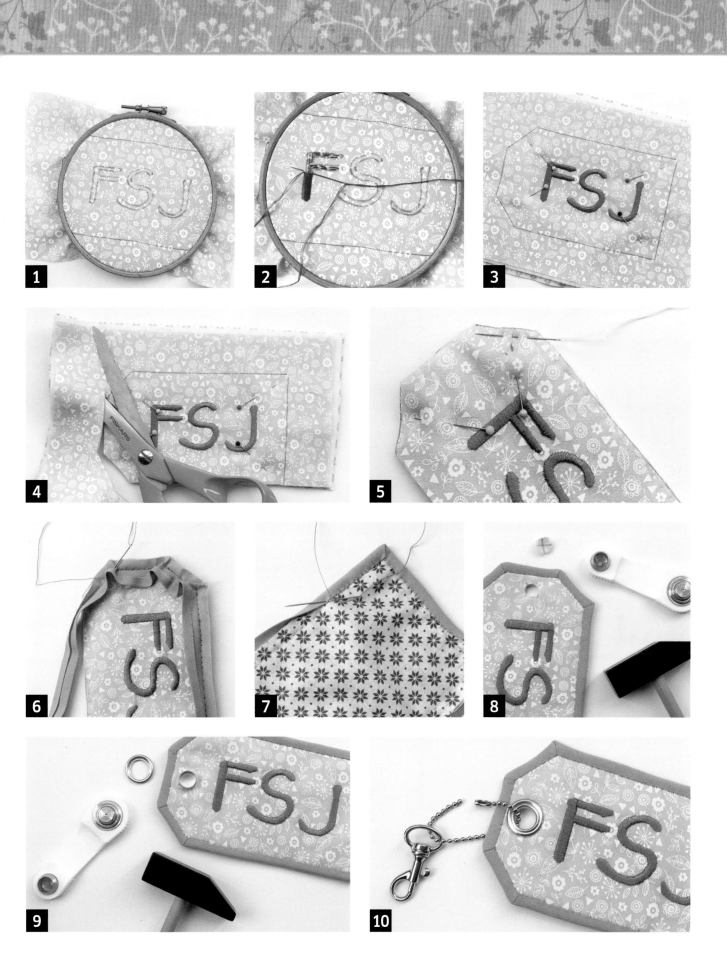

TEMPLATES

Templates shown at actual size can be traced and cut out, or photocopied. For templates reduced in size, enlarge them on an A3 photocopier to the percentage stated.

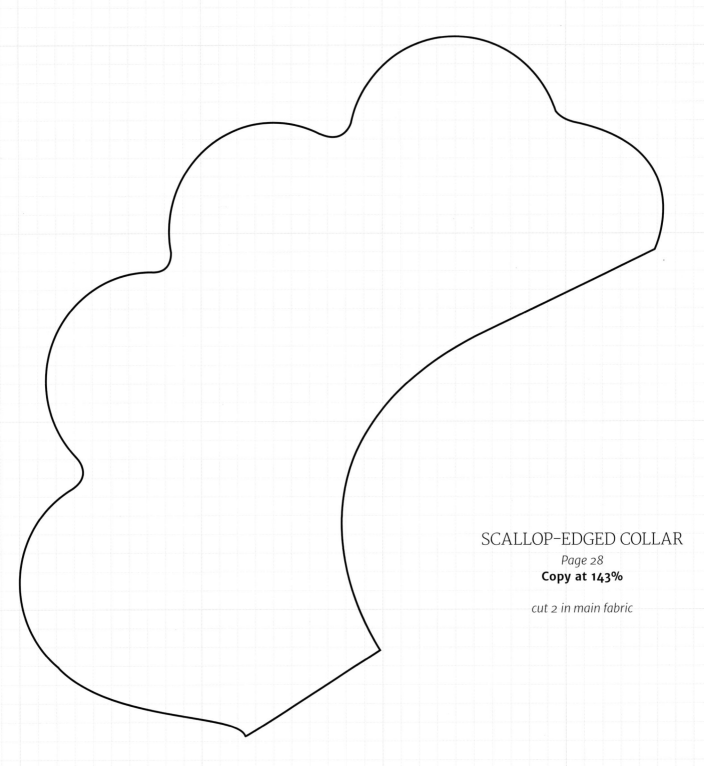

SCALLOP-EDGED COLLAR
Page 28
Copy at 143%

cut 2 in main fabric

SCALLOP-EDGED COLLAR

Page 28
Copy at 143%

cut 2 of each

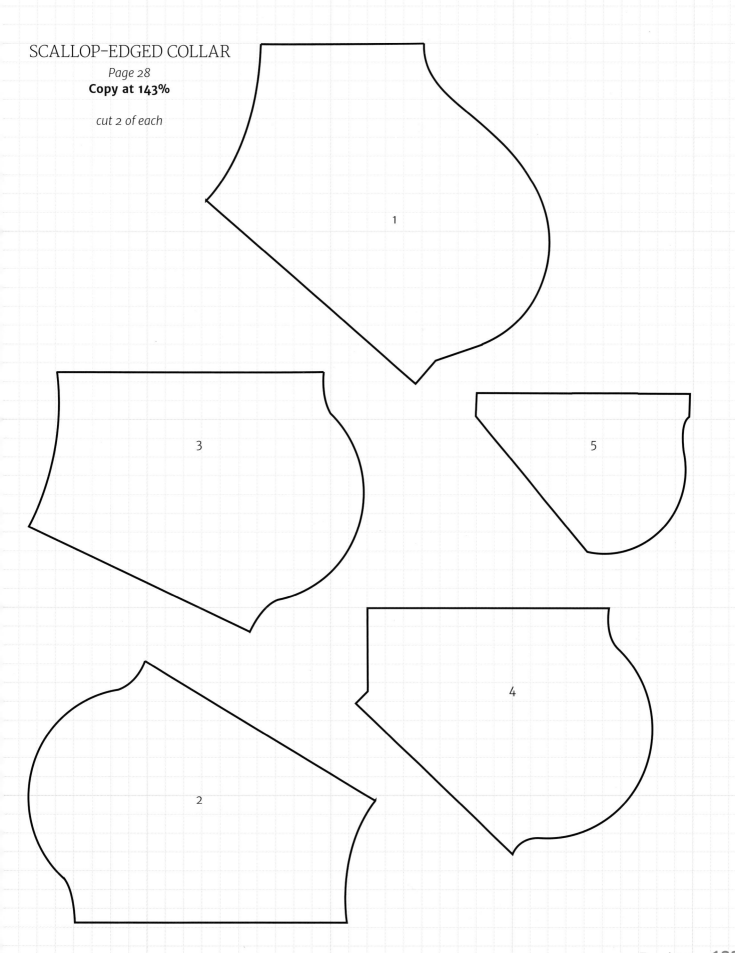

1

3

5

2

4

CLOCHE HAT
Page 54
Copy at 143%

PENDANT
Page 32
Copy at 100%

BRIM
cut 1 in contrast fabric

place broken line on seamline

CLOCHE HAT
Page 54
Copy at 143%

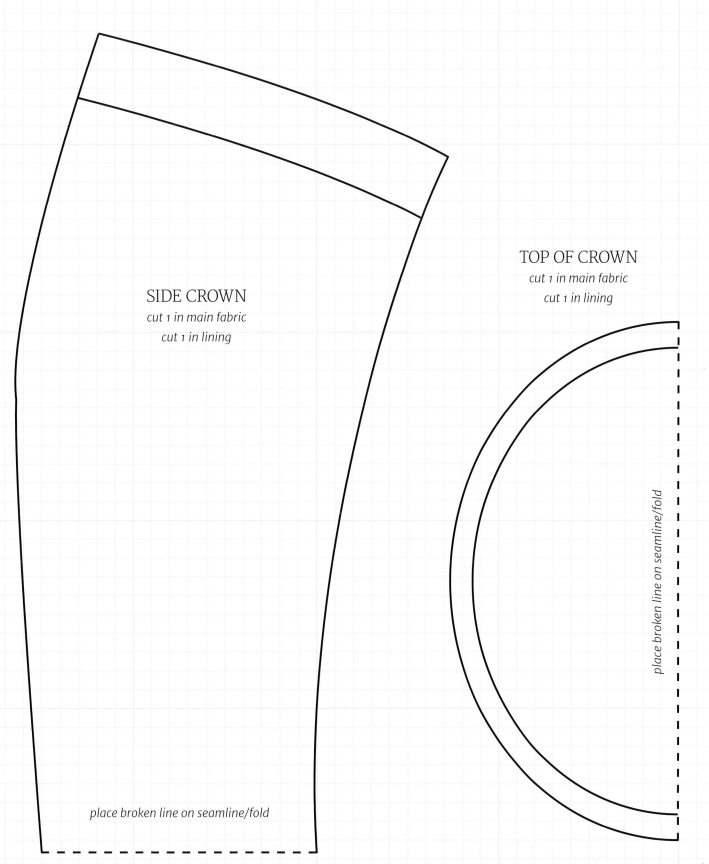

SIDE CROWN
cut 1 in main fabric
cut 1 in lining

TOP OF CROWN
cut 1 in main fabric
cut 1 in lining

place broken line on seamline/fold

place broken line on seamline/fold

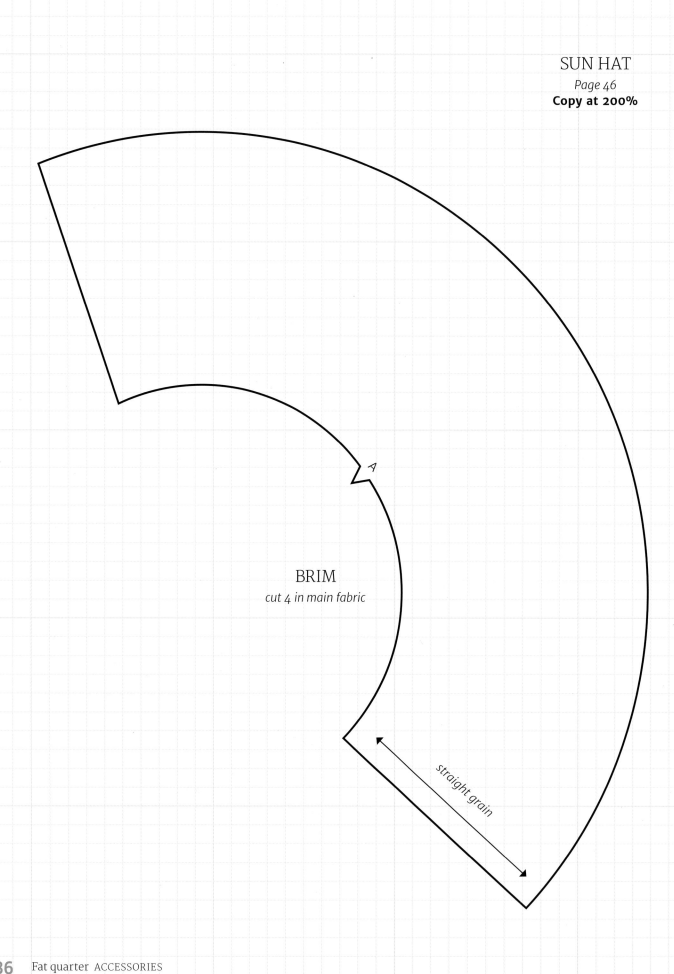

A

BRIM
cut 4 in main fabric

straight grain

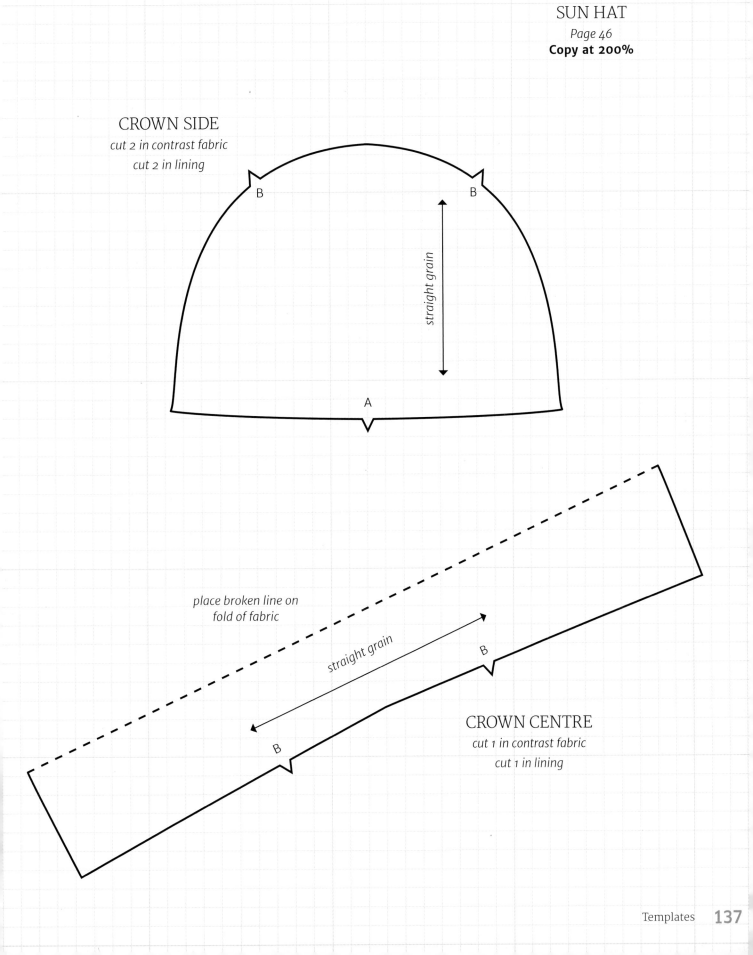

SUN HAT
Page 46
Copy at 200%

CROWN SIDE
cut 2 in contrast fabric
cut 2 in lining

B

B

straight grain

A

*place broken line on
fold of fabric*

straight grain

B

B

CROWN CENTRE
cut 1 in contrast fabric
cut 1 in lining

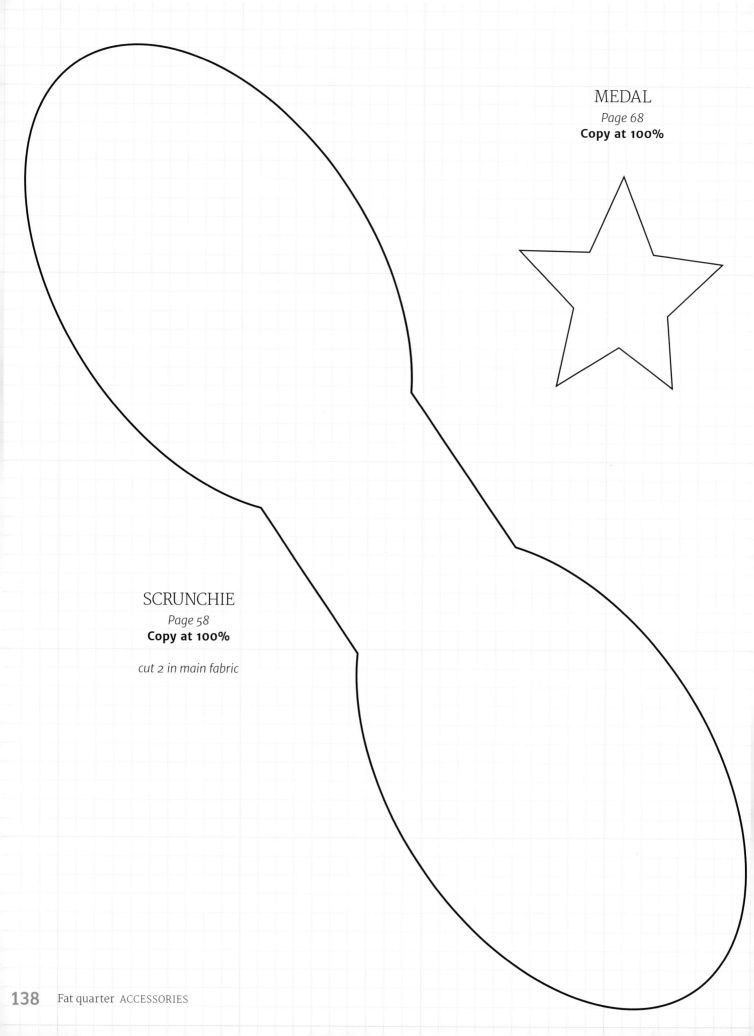

MEDAL

Page 68

Copy at 100%

SCRUNCHIE

Page 58

Copy at 100%

cut 2 in main fabric

VALENTINE BROOCH
Page 72
Copy at 100%

BUTTERFLY BROOCH
Page 80
Copy at 100%

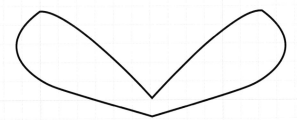

cut 1 each from 2 different silk fabrics

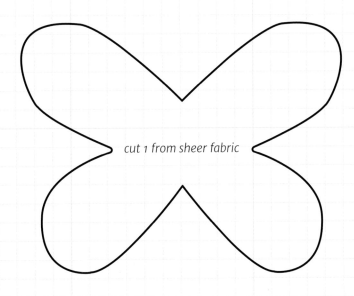

cut 1 from sheer fabric

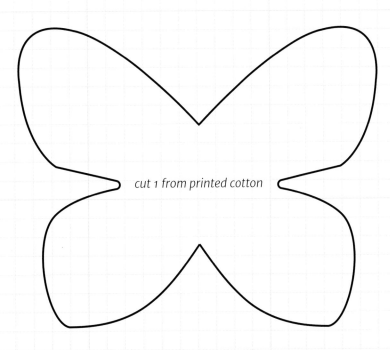

cut 1 from printed cotton

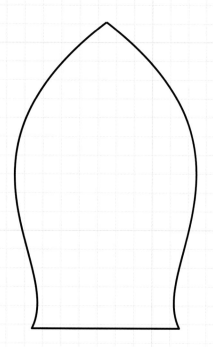

FLOWER CORSAGE
Page 84
Copy at 100%

cut 8

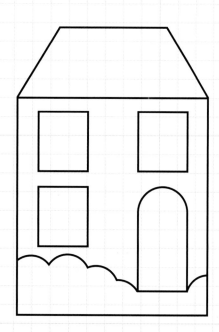

KEY FOB
Page 124
Copy at 100%

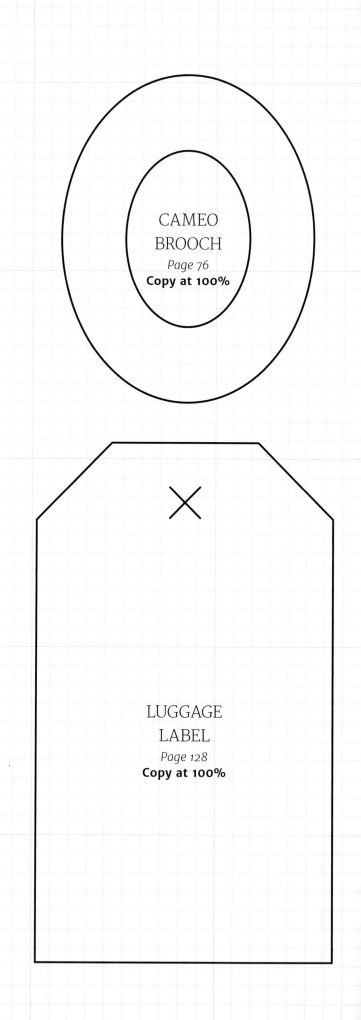

CAMEO
BROOCH
Page 76
Copy at 100%

LUGGAGE
LABEL
Page 128
Copy at 100%

ABCD
EFGH
IJKLM
NOPQR
STUVW
XYZ

RESOURCES

Cotton fabrics, fat quarters
and sewing supplies
www.cottonpatch.co.uk
www.craftcotton.com
www.fabricland.co.uk

Photo fabric cotton poplin
www.cottonpatch.co.uk

Embroidery threads
www.cloudcraft.co.uk

Sewing machines and accessories
www.jaycotts.co.uk

General haberdashery
www.sewandsew.co.uk

Beads and findings
www.beadsdirect.co.uk

Shoe clips
www.amazon.com

Sinamay hat bases and feathers
www.macculloch-wallis.co.uk

ACKNOWLEDGEMENTS

Many thanks to Jonathan Bailey for asking me to write this book,
to Dominique Page, Senior Project Editor, for her patience and
helpfulness, to Sarah Hoggett for editing the text so skilfully,
and to Wayne Blades for directing the styled photography and
for designing such attractive pages. Thanks also to my Mum
for teaching me to sew in the first place, and to my daughters,
Lillie and Edith, for their advice and input.

INDEX

To order a book, or to request
a catalogue, contact:

GMC Publications Ltd
Castle Place, 166 High Street,
Lewes, East Sussex,
BN7 1XU
United Kingdom
Tel: +44 (0)1273 488005
www.gmcbooks.com